The TREES of
SOUTH FLORIDA

FRANK C. CRAIGHEAD, SR.

⇜The TREES of
SOUTH FLORIDA

Volume I

The Natural Environments
and Their Succession

Published in cooperation with the
Everglades Natural History Association

University of Miami Press ⦿
Coral Gables, Florida

Copyright © 1971 by
University of Miami Press
Library of Congress Catalog Card Number 75-107362
ISBN 0-87024-146-X

Second printing 1972

Designed by Mary Lipson

Manufactured in the United States of America

Contents

Illustrations

To Daniel Beard

Preface

This volume presents information pertaining to the numerous plant communities of South Florida. Many of these were described by the early botanists, particularly Harper and Small. These men lived in the area a great part of their lives and wrote with much understanding.

It attempts to point out the interrelations of these plant communities and their changes under the influences of various climatic and edaphic pressures, such as the rising sea, hurricanes, salinity, fire, frost, fresh water variations, as well as others. The intimate relationship between animals and plants such as found in the "gator hole ecosystem," the land-building properties of the mangroves and the periphyton mats is pointed out.

This is often called a unique country. It can be rough as well, and one soon learns to regard it with respect. Prior to coming to live in South Florida in 1950, my work carried me into practically all of the forest communities of the United States and eastern Canada. Soon after my arrival in the land of the Everglades, it became evident that getting about in these extensive swamps was a considerable problem in logistics. In fact, I soon rated the area as one of the most formidable of our natural environments. At that time glade buggies were developing, airboats were just coming into practical use, and that remarkable conveyance the Seminole dugout was passing. One "cracker" told me of several attempts to construct a swamp "snowshoe" or ski for hunting expeditions. There have been many contrivances rigged on the end of a push pole to prevent the pole from sinking too deeply into the mud, in which case on retrieval all momentum of the boat is lost, or the pusher may even be thrown out bodily.

During the rainy season, airboats are useful in the freshwater swamps, but they are useless in the mangroves or where pinnacle rock is present. A canoe or glades skiff propelled by pole, or occasionally even by sail, proves excellent transportation during high water. During the ever-lengthening dry season resulting from the increasing drainage of the surface waters, pushing a canoe or skiff through stands of saw grass is impossible. The helicopter equipped with skis or floats is probably the most efficient conveyance for close inspection of some areas, but there are many places where pilots will not land because of limestone spurs, too much brush, or where the swamp is too boggy. In time one learns to rely on shanks' mare for close study of most of the environments, even though walking is a time-consuming method. In the late dry season when the sticky marls have hardened, travel by foot is permissible on certain relatively smooth terrain such as thin stands of saw grass and spike rush glades. In areas where solution holes are abundant or where pinnacle rock is prominent among the saw grass, however, walking is out of the question except after fires when one can see the pitfalls and shorten or lengthen his stride in order to step on the flat spots. Some of the deeper erosion patterns are such that crossing certain areas requires climbing down onto the mud floor of a solution hole and then up the opposite side. Much of this highly riddled limestone is eroded below more than the surface indicates, resulting in fragile cones that snap and topple under the least pressure.

The deep, wide swamps between the larger estuaries are practically impossible to walk through even after fires have burned off the vegetation. Where juncus, saw grass, or fringe sedges provide a mass of rhizomes forming a firm surface, one can proceed with caution. These flats are often broken with innumerable ponds of liver mud, which often have floating rims that may suddenly drop off 6 to 9 feet to bedrock. A strong pole, therefore, is a useful tool to have when attempting to cross these swampy flats on foot.

The mangrove flats—I speak now of those composed largely of black and white mangroves—are relatively easy to slosh through at low tide when there is no salt water except that mixed in a shallow layer of ooze. Where red mangrove forms a considerable proportion of the forest, their prop roots truly form an "iron curtain." Here it is a matter of chopping a tunnel through a network of prop roots that may be up to 8 feet or more in height. Otherwise, one must resort to twisting and turning until every muscle in one's body aches.

Tramping from Lostman's River to Johnson Mound, about one and one-half miles as the crow flies, takes about three hours. Night travel anywhere on foot is not to be considered. After some experience in tramping one learns that the worst pinnacle rock fosters scrubby buttonwood. In the pineland sloughs and glades, short grasses make for easy going. Bumelia and buttonbush are indicative of a drainage that usually presents a smooth marl soil.

In canoeing in the larger sloughs, one learns to recognize the deeper water by the taller saw grass and beak rushes, and thereby knows how to keep out of shoals. Nothing is more discouraging than having to drag a loaded canoe through saw grass growing in pinnacle rock.

These cautionary words are not meant to discourage would-be explorers. By learning about the variety of fascinating habitats of the area, many safe and satisfying trips can be had. These volumes have been written in part to provide background information that will be helpful. Volume I presents descriptions of the many natural environments and the plants that play roles in shaping them.

In Volume II, trees are described specifically in such a way as to separate each from its associates when considered with its habits and habitats. Employing a minimum of technical terms, emphasis is placed on distinctive characteristics that are conspicuous throughout much of the year—leaves, fruit, flowers, bark, roots, or form, as the case may be—to most readily serve to speed field identification.

The plants are mentioned in this volume under the physiographic provinces. Many plant communities have been referred to by common names in local usage in South

Florida. The plant names also are often local terms and should not be confused with plants by similar common names in other areas. For this reason, in some instances a scientific name has been used in place of the local name in order to more precisely describe the plant in question. For verification of the exact genus and species, refer to the index of common and scientific names.

This work spans a period of twenty years of continuous study of the area. Prior to this period, I had visited the Everglades National Park first in 1917, and thereafter I had frequently visited timber lands in other parts of Florida. Immediately after Hurricane Donna in 1960, sixty-five study plots of one or two square chains were established in the storm path both in saline and freshwater areas. I have observed these plots several times each year for ten years. The vegetation was mapped in many and all were photographed from the air and ground. Gradually, these first studies were extended into all the plant communities of Dade, Collier, and Monroe counties. Some of the areas studied have been observed annually and some only at longer intervals. The basic work on this manuscript was completed in 1968, and though some changes have been made recently, it does not reflect in all respects the current status of the area.

The reader should keep in mind that profound changes are underway in this region, changes both from natural and man-made sources. It is hoped that the present trend to halt the destruction of these environments is not too late to save many of them for posterity.

Acknowledgments

I am greatly indebted to a number of people who have assisted in my studies in South Florida over the past twenty years. First I wish to express my appreciation to the many rangers, unnamed here, of the Everglades National Park who have helped immensely in getting me about this difficult terrain and into the backcountry. Management Biologist Richard W. Klukas has been most helpful on field trips for several years, and our discussions often centered around the application of these studies to management policies of the Park. A collaborator's appointment with the Everglades National Park has provided me with field assistance and has deferred my travel expenses for the past ten years.

Several geologists working in the Park from time to time have been helpful in the interpretation of sedimentation and the effects of the rising sea. I wish to thank Dr. R. N. Ginsburg of the University of Miami Rosenstiel Institute of Marine and Atmospheric Science; Dr. William G. Smith, Department of Geology, Pennsylvania State University; and Dr. David W. Scholl, U.S. Geological Survey, Menlo Park, California. Dr. Scholl worked closely with me on his several field trips into the Park while collecting cores for his studies of the rising sea. References to the ages of various strata are based on radiocarbon dating from the samples we collected, which were processed by Dr. Minze Stuiver, Radiocarbon Laboratory, Yale University.

Dr. P. B. Tomlinson of the Fairchild Tropical Garden has accompanied me on many field trips in this area during the past six years. His assistance in reading the manuscript is greatly appreciated.

The Committee for Research and Exploration of the National Geographic Society has collaborated in these studies for the past five years. Most of the photographs used in these volumes were prepared in the Society's photographic laboratory.

I am grateful to Dr. Daniel B. Ward of the University of Florida, whose checklists I have used for the scientific names of the trees described in these volumes.

Dr. J. D. Dalton of the Dade County Extension Service has assisted with salinity determinations and analyses of numerous water and soil samples collected in the area. Mr. W. R. Llewellyn, formerly of the same service, helped materially with his unpublished reports on local soils and salinity conditions.

I am especially indebted to my companion on many field trips, Mr. Glenn Simmons of Florida City, Florida.

F. C. Craighead

Homestead, Florida
May, 1971

The TREES of
SOUTH FLORIDA

Introduction

Southern Florida, characterized by a subtropical climate, is unusually rich botanically. A major portion of the flora originated in the tropics, most of it in the West Indies, and several species of trees came into the area from the north temperate zone. Since white man arrived, a number of species from other parts of the world have become established. Several are becoming serious weeds. Already over much of subtropical Florida extensive diking, canalization, bulkheading, building, and farming have brought profound changes, often completely destroying the original environment. Many of the original plant communities revert to weed species, largely exotic, rather than to native vegetation after their abandonment for agricultural purposes.

The specific area covered in these volumes is restricted to the three southernmost counties—Collier, Dade, and Monroe—and most of it lies south of the Tamiami Trail (Fig. 1). It includes all of the mainland comprising the tip of Florida; its offshore islands; the Florida Keys; and Florida Bay with its more than 100 islands. It does not include the subtropical coastal strips extending some miles farther north along the east and west coasts of Florida.

The region covered here is in a large part a new land. This is true not only historically but geologically as well. Its modern history dates back nearly 400 years, and its pre-Columbian human history is thought to be about 2,000 years older. Nearly one-fifth of the present land surface of the three-county area—the mangrove zone and part of the freshwater swamps—has been formed within the past four to five thousand years.

Early generations of aborigines, the Tequesta and the Calusa Indians, lived on numerous coastal shell mounds lapped by the waters of Florida Bay and the Gulf of Mexico. These mounds were usually near oyster bars at the mouth of estuaries. As the land built up under the influence of a rising sea, new shorelines formed seaward, and the space between the homesites of the Indians and the food supply gradually widened. The present shoreline is now a mile or two seaward from many of the larger mounds. The bases of some of the mounds occupied by these Indians, who vanished shortly after the Spanish arrived, are now covered with 2 or more feet of sediment laid down since their early occupation.

At other places, as off the deltas of the Shark and Broad rivers, the shoreline has receded one-half to one mile with the rising sea. It would be of interest to probe some of the shoals off these coasts for evidence of older Indian middens.

Until white men with little foresight changed the situation, the plants and animals of the area were adjusted to the physical forces and formed many remarkable ecosystems, according to descriptions by the earliest naturalists. True, there were storms, droughts, and fires that left their record in dead trees and logs in the hammocks and in layers of ashes in peat beds. Locally these did much damage. Overall, however, the hurricanes prepared the land for new mangrove forests, and the fires maintained the pine woods and great savannahs of saw grass. Man's decision to disturb all of this for his own needs drastically changed the entire ecology of the area.

Concerted efforts were begun early in the century to conserve the unique biological treasures of the Everglades area. The Florida Federation of Women's Clubs in 1916 dedicated the Royal Palm State Park. The Everglades National Park was formally dedicated in 1947. Its final boundaries, encompassing about 1,288,500 acres of land and its surrounding waters, were not finally determined until 1958. The 858,500 acres of land in the Park are critically affected by conditions in the rest of southern Florida, especially by the altered water situation.

Daniel B. Beard was chosen in 1937 to make a biological survey of the Everglades and estuarine swamps of South Florida to determine their suitability for a national park and also to propose its natural boundaries. Dan, an excellent biologist and field man, spent over 4 years studying the area and its plants and animals. He was appointed the first superintendent of Everglades National Park in 1947 and efficiently managed the area for the following 13 years. Had his recommendations for natural boundaries of the Park been adopted and his management policies been followed after his transfer to Washington in 1959, many of the Park's present problems might have been avoided.

Recently, national attention has been focused on the area of the Everglades National Park and its threatened future. To better understand the present complicated situation, it seems useful to review briefly the history of man's ditching and diking in southern Florida. In 1881, Hamilton Disston purchased four million acres of "Everglades" land at twenty-five cents an acre for the purpose of opening and developing much of peninsular Florida. His early drainage project in the Kissimmee-Caloosahatchee-Okeechobee complex caused the first reduction of water in Lake Okeechobee, whose waters occasionally overflowed into the great Everglades swamp.

More vital changes began in 1913 and increased through 1918 as canals from the east coast reached Lake Okeechobee and moved fresh water to the ocean. Some of the rivers, notably the Miami, the North, the New, and the Hillsboro, drew water from the Everglades that once fed the Shark River Slough. In 1928 the Tamiami Trail was completed. Despite culverts designed to allow the natural water flow to continue, the roadway considerably restricted the water flow into the eastern portion of what is now Everglades National Park (Johnson, 1958).

As the canals to Lake Okeechobee were completed, Conservation Areas 1, 2, and 3 were set up to provide reservoirs and water for the diminishing wildlife. At the same time, population pressure demanded more and more dry land for homesites, and farmers cleared more and more land to meet the increasing demand for winter vegetables. During this early farming period, which demanded comprehensive adjustments to new conditions, there were many crop and financial failures from flooding, frosts, and in good years from overproduction for the existing market. The early glade farmers wanted drainage to prevent winter flooding of their crops. Later, about 1950, after machinery was developed to clear and grind up the rocky pinelands, another type of farming came into dominance. These new "rock farmers" wanted some drainage but not too much. All the while, the realtors backed both types of farmers because cleared and dry land was easier for them to sell. Since standing water in the pines from heavy downpours could occur at almost any time during the tourist season, man-made drainage efforts were welcomed by realtors.

In short, nature's drainage system for the pineland through its transverse saw grass sloughs was insufficient for the impatient farmers and realtors. To meet their demands, numerous deep canals were cut across the pineland ridge from the Everglades on the west to Biscayne Bay on the east (Fig. 1). These canals lowered the water table 4 to 5 feet around and west of Homestead, and the effects were extended several miles farther to lower the water table that maintained Taylor Slough and much of the pineland in the Everglades National Park.

Between 1915 and 1920 several canals were dredged inland to the Park from Florida Bay or the Gulf of Mexico across the mangroves into certain interior ponds or flats. These included Slagle's and House's ditches, the Homestead Canal from Paradise Key to Cape Sable, East and Middle Cape canals, and a ditch leading into Lostman's River. Later, the Buttonwood Canal from Flamingo to Coot Bay was constructed. Only the Homestead Canal tapped the large, interior, freshwater basin. The others opened into shallow marl flats behind the coastal embankment. These flats held fresh water during the rainy season and were reported to contain bigmouth bass as well as some adaptable marine fish (such as tarpon and redfish) that came in with hurricanes.

Salt water quickly changed the fauna of these ponds and flats and greatly altered the vegetation on the surrounding land. Serious erosion at the mouth of these canals in the coastal embankment followed their construction. The canals

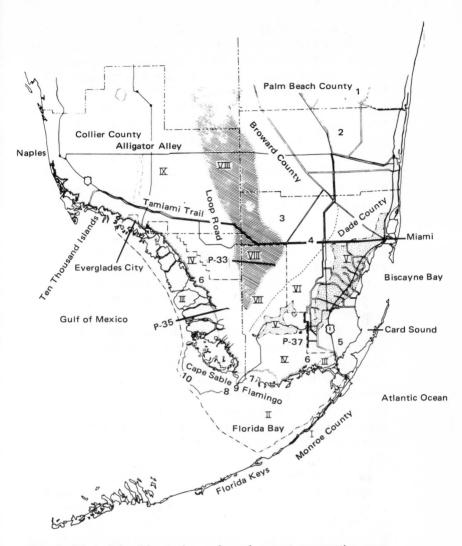

Fig. 1. Principal localities, early canals, and present conservation areas. *(1) Conservation Area 1; (2) Conservation Area 2; (3) Conservation Area 3; (4) Canal 67; (5) Canal C-111; (6) Buttonwood Embankment; (7) Buttonwood Canal; (8) East Cape Canal; (9) Slagle's and House's Ditches; (10) Middle Cape Canal. Gauging stations are indicated by P-33, P-35, and P-37. Dot and dash line (—·—·—) marks Everglades National Park boundaries. Roman numerals indicate Physiographic Provinces (see Fig. 7, p. 78).*

were dug, ostensibly, to promote the sale of surrounding land for agriculture and for homesites. They accomplished neither, but many lots were sold that are perpetually flooded by the introduced tides. Superintendent Daniel B. Beard attempted to close three of these canals in 1955. Maintenance on the dams was neglected, and they were subsequently badly damaged by hurricanes before the vegetation became established on them.

In 1956 and 1957 the Buttonwood Canal from Flamingo to Coot Bay was constructed, letting the highly saline waters of Florida Bay into this large freshwater pond. The aquatic flora that had supported a magnificent coot and duck display was immediately destroyed, and the birds left this feeding ground. A channel cut from West Lake through Long and Cuthbert lakes about the same time likewise permitted salt water to reach the western end of West Lake and destroy another rich winter feeding ground. The construction of both of these canals was also opposed by Superintendent Beard.

Outside the Park boundaries, the glade farmers planted more and more lowlands to the west and east of the pineland ridge, the rock farmers got a much longer planting season and bought more irrigation pumps, and the realtors blocked out new developments. The hunters who kill "aquatic" deer from airboats in the areas to the north got questionable compensation from a million dollars worth of high water refuges, locally called deer islands, along the new Miami Canal.

The beginnings of these changes were perceived and documented by early naturalists (Small, 1929; Simpson, 1932; Barbour, 1944), but their warnings fell on deaf ears. As time passed it became evident that one set of alterations brought about changes that needed further adjustments, and so on—until the situation became so complex that no one understood it. The conservationists are now told that water will be supplied from Lake Okeechobee 100 miles to the north at a price, to be paid by public funds, of some 250 million dollars or more for enlarging that reservoir. To the writer, once himself a farmer, too many factors are still uncontrolled to promise a better future. Too many beans, tomatoes, and potatoes can still glut the market and make harvests unprofitable. The freezes that sweep down with the "northers" periodically continue, and are possibly worse as the dry winters lengthen. Natural droughts coinciding with the ever-increasing demand for water allocations for industrial and agricultural uses will still continue to shortchange our wildlife. Conservationists hope that the developers' slogan, "Is the water for man or for the birds and the alligators? " will gradually have less influence on land-use decisions.

Someday, let us hope, man may realize—before it is too late—that he cannot live here and destroy the natural environments of this remarkable land. Instead of a vast system of canals, dikes, concrete strips, and high rises covering southern Florida in the future, we must plan now for intelligent land use. Man can still confine his construction and farming to the higher lands on both coasts and preserve the great interior swamps and mangrove estuaries for the fishes, birds, and alligators. Thus he may still retain the amenities of these wild lands for his own enjoyment and for others to enjoy in the future.

The Everglades National Park can never be restored to its former glories, but much can be saved if we can prevent the destruction of the interior freshwater swamps of this great ecosystem. The plant communities will change drastically under the present water regulations. High land will become continuous forest, with xerophitic trees predominating. Much of the cypress will disappear, and many of the saw grass communities will become swamp hardwood forests. There will be accompanying changes in the wildlife as feeding grounds are shifted or destroyed. Many rookeries will disappear. And even the alligator, instead of increasing with fewer poachers, may have to survive in artificial ponds blasted out of the bedrock. In the interest of preserving those natural communities that are left, their diverse and in many cases unique characteristics are described in this volume with emphasis on the woody plants as typifying these sites and their recent changes.

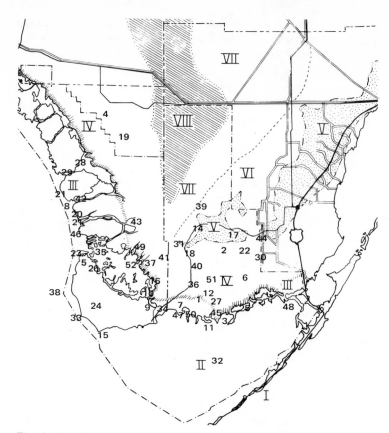

Fig. 2. Specific sites noted in text. *Locations are approximate because of limitations of map size.*

1 Alligator Creek	19 Gum Slough	36 Nine Mile Pond
2 Atoll Hammock	20 Harney River	37 North River
3 Big Madeira Bay	21 Highland Beach	38 Northwest Cape
4 Big Pine Island	22 Ingraham Highway	39 Pahayokee
5 Big Sable Creek	23 Joe River	40 Paurotis Pond
6 Big Thicket	24 Lake Ingraham	41 Roberts River
7 Black Forest	25 Little Madeira Bay	42 Rodgers River
8 Broad River	26 Little Sable Creek	43 Rookery Branch
9 Cactus Point	27 Long Lake	44 Royal Palm Hammock
10 Coot Bay	28 Lostman's Creek	(Paradise Key)
11 Crocodile Point	29 Lostman's River	45 Seven Palm Lake
12 Cuthbert Lake	30 Madeira Slough	46 Shark River
13 Dead-end Pond	(Taylor Slough)	47 Snake Bight
14 Dwarf Cypress Pond	31 Mahogany Hammock	48 Snipe Point
15 East Cape	32 Man O' War Key	49 Watson River
16 East River	33 Middle Cape	50 West Lake
17 Farm Road	34 Mrazek Pond	51 Whiskey Creek
18 Flamingo Road	35 Mud Lake	52 Whitewater Bay

1 ❧ Climate and Tree Growth

The three southern counties of Florida lie south of 25 degrees north latitude and enjoy a subtropical climate with temperature means varying only around 15 degrees Fahrenheit between summer highs and winter lows. Rainfall is seasonal; from 60 to 80 percent of the annual precipitation usually falls in a five month period from May through October. Scattered showers break the winter dry season with averages of 1 to 2 inches of rainfall per month. Some years the winter rainfall is negligible. Four weather stations have been maintained in Everglades National Park for over fifteen years. Annual precipitation at these stations, plus one at Homestead, are shown in one table. Another table presents monthly precipitation at Homestead (pp. 10, 11).

This "tropical savannah" type of climate (Hela, 1952), with its alternate wet and dry seasons, is normally highly favorable to luxuriant plant growth and abundant animal life. The growth of green plant material during the rainy season is phenomenal. This green vegetation is partly preserved where swampy conditions are maintained, but where the waters recede part of this organic matter is broken down (by oxidation and the action of bacteria and fungi) into simpler compounds, and thus it is made available to other plants and animals. These living organisms are remarkably adjusted to the normal extremes, and it is only when these values are exceeded during hurricanes, excessive droughts, and freezes that severe disturbances result.

Some of the unique biological adjustments resulting from the climate and the edaphic factors of this region may be

Annual Precipitation at Five South Florida Stations

Year	Homestead Experiment Station	Everglades City	Tamiami (40 Mile Bend)	Royal Palm Ranger Station	Flamingo
1940	70.37	54.69	–	–	–
1941	76.47	–	–	–	–
1942	63.31	36.59	–	–	–
1943	56.80	40.64	58.96	–	–
1944	51.15	42.24	41.60	–	–
1945	54.28	57.42	53.55	–	–
1946	64.27	56.27	46.70	–	–
1947	94.07	78.19	82.76	–	–
1948	70.57	57.49	58.47	–	–
1949	65.32	–	69.26	–	–
1950	55.96	44.26	56.96	–	–
1951	45.64	37.50	38.39	–	30.88
1952	58.24	58.77	56.34	48.75	45.92
1953	63.99	62.01	63.49	54.76	63.51
1954	67.76	64.35	49.99	64.10	53.48
1955	52.59	50.48	46.13	47.30	37.18
1956	45.37	39.92	42.97	28.72	26.18
1957	63.22	50.51	68.22	48.26	51.18
1958	73.00	75.10	59.33	70.46	62.41
1959	87.09	64.29	67.18	76.92	60.23
1960	82.12	67.32	73.91	70.52	69.74
1961	45.75	41.43	44.05	36.52	24.36
1962	55.56	56.89	56.06	51.16	43.27
1963	62.65	52.72	62.41	53.57	41.90
1964	61.09	50.34	55.28	62.78	39.35
1965	46.30	43.92	49.49	49.86	42.00
1966	59.99	63.76	61.46	73.00	66.02
1967	54.15	45.57	53.52	55.97	45.49
1968	83.67	69.33	66.84	95.26	70.10
1969	83.72	63.61	75.11	83.75	69.68
Average	63.48	40.14	42.12	58.75	49.62

seen in the mangrove forests that flourish under alternate baths of fresh and salt water and provide a nursery ground for much marine life; in the tropical hardwood hammocks that provide a mild microclimate of high humidity and frost-free temperatures suitable to a tropical flora of trees, ferns, orchids, and bromeliads; in the pineland forests of the rock land that support more than 100 endemic plants

Year	Jan	Feb	Mar	Apr	May	June	July	Aug	Sept	Oct	Nov	Dec
1950	0.27	0.61	0.78	3.22	7.95	2.33	9.05	7.78	7.78	11.88	1.10	3.21
1951	0.18	2.43	0.28	4.54	3.13	3.54	12.11	7.15	5.81	5.60	0.74	0.13
1952	0.47	3.34	6.86	2.20	3.31	3.82	10.35	11.41	5.37	9.68	0.75	0.68
1953	4.21	1.73	0.60	3.83	2.82	16.11	7.73	5.20	6.91	11.25	2.91	0.69
1954	0.71	2.88	2.77	7.77	11.94	9.26	10.39	5.98	8.58	5.53	1.30	0.65
1955	0.95	0.82	0.35	2.42	3.95	11.57	5.63	8.46	8.74	6.80	1.12	1.78
1956	1.21	1.14	0.00	3.06	5.67	2.63	4.06	8.65	8.87	8.11	1.01	0.96
1957	0.77	4.65	3.31	7.90	5.21	3.80	7.32	13.08	6.15	6.96	1.09	2.98
1958	5.51	1.29	6.12	0.35	18.60	6.29	11.46	5.20	5.02	7.66	2.05	3.45
1959	1.19	2.99	7.27	2.59	7.46	14.41	10.59	6.28	10.32	13.04	9.72	1.23
1960	0.20	1.84	0.64	7.44	7.04	13.52	13.90	9.49	19.04	6.79	1.69	0.53
1961	2.54	0.99	3.66	0.04	9.23	10.47	3.08	6.01	2.71	6.02	0.90	0.10
1962	1.42	0.68	4.02	1.37	1.10	14.39	8.43	9.08	9.01	3.56	2.33	0.17
1963	0.50	3.04	0.52	0.57	9.09	10.82	3.51	6.58	20.26	3.56	1.55	2.65
1964	0.55	2.46	1.83	6.16	2.22	9.21	7.09	7.81	8.17	12.11	1.93	1.55
1965	1.96	1.55	1.98	0.19	0.19	5.86	4.14	4.34	12.98	10.85	2.14	0.12
1966	4.58	1.07	3.25	2.24	7.62	17.69	6.35	3.67	7.32	4.78	0.46	0.96
1967	2.66	1.09	3.05	0.27	2.94	16.17	5.63	4.74	7.79	6.03	2.41	1.37
1968	1.22	2.01	0.56	0.40	15.62	23.98	8.60	6.83	13.18	10.40	0.73	0.14
1969	4.72	1.76	2.88	3.40	4.14	20.67	5.78	12.30	11.01	15.52	0.82	0.72
Avg	1.79	1.91	2.53	2.99	6.46	10.82	7.76	7.50	9.25	8.30	1.83	1.40

adapted to the fires of the dry periods; in the abundant life of the solution holes and the gator holes; and in the bird and animal life of the various types of swamps and glades and shell mounds formerly populated by the Indians who lived on the edge of the mangrove coast.

Nowhere else in all our land can be found so many adaptations between such a complex of physical forces and varied biota. Much of this condition, furthermore, has come to pass over several thousand square miles of new land—land that was nonexistent 5,000 years ago.

Hurricanes

The effect of hurricanes on the vegetation of southern Florida has been discussed by numerous scientists (Davis, 1940; Egler, 1952; Craighead and Gilbert, 1962; Craighead, 1964; Alexander, 1967; and Perkins, 1968). Although the writer had noted such local effects of past hurricanes on the

Mature mangrove. *A stand of red, white, and black mangroves photographed in 1920 when the Homestead Canal was being built (from Holt and Sutton, 1926). This stand was known as the Black Forest by early Flamingo residents. Many of the trees were over 3 feet in diameter and were about 250 years of age. Data on tree ages are based on radiocarbon datings by the School of Atmospheric and Marine Science, University of Miami, and also by the diameter increments compared with those of a stand of second-growth mangroves on the same site known to be 25 years old.*

vegetation as windfalls and the stubs of bygone mangrove forests, it was not until Hurricane Donna passed over the area on September 7, 1960, that the full portent of the power and the resulting devastation wrought by these storms was realized.

The total elimination of a massive mangrove forest is illustrated by the series of five spaced pictures taken from 1920 through 1969 on Hurricane Donna Study Plot 10 near Flamingo.

Two severe hurricanes have completely altered the character of the mangrove forests on the tip of Florida. The Labor Day hurricane of September 1, 1935, devastated all of the mature stands of mangrove in the eastern portions of the Park to Cape Sable. It did little damage to the mangroves in the Shark River system and north to Marco. Hurricane Donna covered the entire mangrove belt from Little Madeira Bay to Fort Myers.

In certain places, particularly in stands of second-growth red mangrove, the trees were sheared off completely. This was attributed to tornado-like winds within the storm wall (Craighead and Gilbert, 1962; Dunn and Miller, 1964). In other places, in fact in most of the mature stands in the Park, the mangrove trees were left upright but were stripped of many branches. There remains practically no extensive stand of mature trees anywhere in the area.

The explanation for the sudden and complete mortality of all species in certain areas was puzzling. Practically all species of trees were completely defoliated except the low (up to 3 to 5 feet tall) understory and those trees that were uprooted by the first winds and lay more or less protected on the ground. In contrast to this, epidemics of insects and diseases build up gradually and are usually confined to one or a few species of host trees. A single defoliation by insects or diseases seldom kills a tree. Within two to four weeks after the storm the trees began putting out new growth

Second-growth mangrove stand. *A second-growth stand 25 years of age near Flamingo. This stand was cut through in road building in 1956, and was part of the replacement stand in the Black Forest that was destroyed by the Labor Day hurricane in 1935. These trees were about 35 feet tall and averaged 4 inches in diameter. Red mangroves dominated, and black and white mangroves were also represented.*

Hurricane damage (above). *Hurricane Donna in September 1960 completely killed the second-growth stand and exposed the stubs of the older forest.* Regrowth before Hurricane Betsy (facing page, above). *Taken in May 1964, four months before Hurricane Betsy, this photograph shows the area well covered by red, white, and black mangrove seedlings, with many dead poles from 1960 still standing.* Damage from Hurricane Betsy (facing page, below). *Taken in December 1969 after Hurricane Betsy, this photograph illustrates the destruction of much of the seedling growth of the previous illustration. Weedy plants have become established to form a ground cover of grasses, sedges, cattails, and careless weed that will completely inhibit mangrove reproduction for many years to come. Later, fires will probably destroy such temporary plants in a very dry winter, and flood tides will spread a mixture of mangrove seedlings over the bare ground to reestablish a mangrove forest. Soil profiles show that this has happened several times in the past 4,000 years.*

from adventitious buds. Six weeks later the leaves began to yellow and wither, and ambrosia beetles began attacking the trunks, indicating death of the cambium. On nearby trees growing on slight elevations of 1 foot or more, such as road berms, canal banks, Indian mounds, and coastal embankments, the leaves continued to develop normally. Six weeks after Hurricane Donna, these sites stood out green in a brown landscape of dead and dying plants. Examination of the roots of the affected trees six to eight weeks after the storm showed that all of the small feeding rootlets were already dead and decomposed. High salinity of the trapped tidal waters as they evaporated was not considered as a

Bear Lake Canal (top). *One year after Hurricane Donna had passed, her devastation was still plainly evident. Vast areas were dead, but beneath these trees many new seedlings had started. On the slightly higher elevations along canal banks and on Indian mounds, tropical hardwood communities escaped destruction and were still green. Here the suffocating mud was washed off the flooded base by copious rainfall before the tree roots were killed. Several Indian mounds are visible as slightly darker islands. Bear Lake Canal five years later (bottom). Hurricane damage five years after Hurricane Donna resulted in a complete kill in the low mangrove flat, while the mangrove and other trees growing on the canal embankment survived because the mud blanket was washed off and the roots remained in aerated soil.*

factor in the case of Donna, since this storm was accompanied by over 10 inches of precipitation. (Later, in September 1965, salinity was associated with Hurricane Betsy.) The high concentration of sulphur dioxide in the soil was considered a factor but did not fit the situation. The breaking of the rootlets by the swaying of the trees was also suggested as an explanation for the mortality, but trees growing on slight elevations a few feet away recovered. Finally it was realized that the mortality was confined to the low areas, those a few tenths of a foot above or below sea level on that part of the area on which a deposit of fine, impervious mud (marl) 0.1 to 0.5 feet thick had been deposited on the forest floor by the 10-foot high tide accompanying the storm. The interior hammocks and bay heads not inundated by the storm tides suffered relatively little damage, chiefly defoliation and some windthrow. Thus the most reasonable explanation appeared to be an oxygen deficiency in the rootlets of the completely defoliated trees.

Aside from the destruction of the mangrove forest, many geomorphic changes came about. Beaches were altered; some were built up and extended, others pushed inland 100 feet or more or carried away. Thus new coastal embank-

Hurricane mud (left). *Hurricane Donna played some unexpected pranks. Probably the most disastrous was the transportation and deposition of tons of Florida Bay mud over the land for as much as ten miles inland. This mud formed an impervious blanket 1 to 5 inches thick over all of the coastal area, shutting off oxygen to the shallow root systems of the plants, thus smothering the tiny root hairs and killing the defoliated trees.* Floating islands (right). *Another prank was the lifting of large chunks of red mangrove peat, with the trees intact, and depositing them some distance inland. The red mangrove prop roots held together masses of peat 2 to 3 feet thick and 10 to 15 feet wide. These roots are composed of well-aerated porous tissues that served as flotation devices. Some chunks settled on land, others in shallow lakes.*

Transported peat chunks. *This chunk of red mangrove peat with the trees that formed it was transported over a mile. It came to rest in Mud Lake, where it formed a small island complete with living trees. Hundreds of these transported chunks were noted throughout the path of Hurricane Donna. The two paddles shown are of the same length; one is resting on the lake bottom, the other on the block of peat, indicating the relative thickness of the peat block.*

ments were set up and new impoundments formed that are now colonized by hammock or swamp trees, respectively. The prairies of Cape Sable, except for the grasses and sedges, were swept clean of most of the vegetation that had formed an open cover previous to the hurricane.

Fires

Any serious consideration of the plant communities in this area brings one to the realization that fires are of the greatest importance in the development and survival of many plant communities. Frank E. Egler (1952) aptly expressed the role of fire: "It is my contention that the herbaceous everglade and the surrounding pinelands were born in fires; that they can survive only with fires; that they are dying today because of fires."

The principal result of fire in these southern forests is its effect on stand composition in maintaining the more fire-resistant species. Fire is the most important single factor in perpetuating the pineland by reducing competition by hardwoods. It maintains the sedges and grasses of the glades and it removes the swamp hardwoods that first become established in the numerous small solution holes. Without fire the hardwoods would gradually spread outward as humus accumulates.

During the rainy season, except for drought years, the Everglades are flooded and the pinelands are partially submerged, or at least their numerous solution holes are filled with water. Practically nothing will burn. During the dry season from December through April the surface water gradually disappears and the accumulation of organic matter becomes combustible. For the most part, winter fires consume only the litter on the surface and kill only the stems and tops of the herbs and shrubs above the moist organic layer of humus. Practically all of the plant associations are adapted to survival under such conditions. Indeed,

Broad River fire. *This swamp lying between the Broad and Rodgers rivers burned in August 1965 while there were several inches of water on the soil. It was probably set by poachers during a high wind to clear access to gator holes. The fire burned for two days. Juncus and brown fringe rush* (Fimbristylis castanea) *formed the ground cover, and there were numerous patches of saw grass on the slightly higher elevations and tree islands. The elevated mangrove shoreline that subtends this swamp was not affected by the fire. This area is characteristic of most of the swamps between the large estuaries. The mucky peat varies from 6 to 12 feet deep to bedrock. In some places where the vegetation is thin, these sediments will not sustain a man's weight. Often the basal 2 to 3 feet are composed of the freshwater mud known as Helisoma marl.*

Saw grass fire. *Fire in the saw grass community does little damage when the soil is wet. In fact, it consumes the great accumulation of dead leaf litter and seems to stimulate new sprouts. The plants sprout immediately, and the new crop of leaves acts as a firebreak for several years. At the time of this fire, about 3 inches of water covered the saw grass rhizomes. When the upper peat layers contain little moisture, fire eats deep and destroys the roots. Regeneration of some stands has not yet occurred following certain fires of 1957. Spike rush marshes often replace the saw grass when the peat layer is destroyed, exposing peat or marl subsoil. Saw grass seeds germinate readily on both marl and peat but wither and die during the winter season when the surface of the soil completely dries. This fire occurred on the north shore of West Lake in 1967.*

the great number of endemics—approximately 100 species—found in the pinelands are adaptations to this type of environment. The hammocks with their moist layer of peat, as well as the bay heads and cypress domes growing in deep peat, resist fire until the moisture content of the humus layer becomes quite low—below 30 percent. Then these organic soils do burn, and fire slowly consumes the plant roots imbedded in the smoldering peat.

Modern man's activities have greatly increased the number and the destructiveness of fires. The amount of water held in the region has been greatly reduced through drainage and diversion, intensifying and prolonging the normal dry season. Formerly, on the pinelands around Homestead that have been cleared for agriculture, the water in the topsoil prohibited planting until November. Since

Controlled fires. *Fire in the coastal pinelands of southeastern United States is being used extensively as a silvicultural tool by the wood-using industries in managing the forests of the coastal plain. Light ground fires when the duff contains some moisture kill the hardwood understory that competes with pines for moisture. This photograph illustrates a typical second-growth stand of Dade County pine in the Everglades National Park. The fire was purposely set and directed. It shows the scorched understory of shrubby growth and very little needle burn on the taller pines. Some pines are killed in such prescribed burning, but in general these small pines are remarkably fire-resistant. Such fires maintain pure stands of pines–an important forest type that is disappearing in South Florida under intense fire protection.*

1967 and 1968, with the drainage canals in operation, some crops are planted in late August and early September. More irrigation by pumping is now necessary for these farm crops.

Small damp-soil fires, those which normally burn out during the first night, are often controlled before they cover more than a few acres. Such fires serve a very useful purpose in breaking the continuity of several years' accumulation of flammable material over large areas. When such heavy accumulations do catch fire, control is impossible except under favorable weather conditions; such fires normally burn until put out by heavy rains or wind shifts. Usually severe fires occur late in the dry season, often in May when the surface is extremely dry. Such fires destroy the organic soil in practically all plant communities, often burning deep to destroy the roots of normally fire-resistant species.

Even in the mangrove belt, fire must be ranked as second to hurricanes as the most potent force in shaping the vegetation. Fires are infrequent here because much of the area is at sea level and is periodically flooded. After hurricanes, great quantities of debris cover the ground for several feet. Given a dry season, the frequent strong winds,

Pineland and saw palmetto fires. *This ground fire has destroyed the small hardwood sprouts in the pineland. In the adjacent glade it has burned off the grasses and sedges and the dead leaves on the saw palmettos. The root systems of all of these plants are uninjured and will sprout within a few days. This photograph also illustrates the procumbent stems of saw palmetto* (Serenoa repens) *and its tendency to grow outward from a common center.*

and a spark, these materials burn with terrific heat, destroying all living plants. This happened after the September 1935 hurricane.

Lightning fires have occurred frequently from the time of the occupation by the early Indians until the present time. When white men arrived to settle on the land around 1900, fires were used to clear the land whenever there was an accumulation of material that would burn. Hunters no doubt have appreciated the attraction of deer to burned-over land where the newly sprouting growth provided them an increased abundance of food with high nutrients (Hilman, 1962). This procedure unquestionably was also used by early white settlers as a method of improving feeding grounds. Soil profiles obtained by coring in the mangrove soils show many charcoal pockets dating back over a period of 3,000 years as these lands were building.

Frosts

Frosts are of prime importance in the agricultural activities of the area. Frost warnings are issued throughout the winter as part of the services of the U.S. Weather Bureau. These reports make front page items in the local newspapers and accurately describe the effects of local freezes on the various crops.

Frosts occur somewhere in the region about every other year. The areas of damage seem to be more extensive now than before drainage. The "scorching" from the frost of February 1, 1966, was sharply defined on buttonwood and coco plum along a line between the wet and dry glades.

Severe frosts have a considerable influence on stand composition and tree distribution here. Buttonwood and all three species of mangrove are severely injured by temperatures of 30 degrees Fahrenheit. White mangrove and buttonwood are most susceptible, red less so, and black least; the latter has not been killed in the Park by freezes of the past fifteen years. Buttonwood and coco plum both grow far inland in the glades and are regularly cut back to their persistent root systems to form many-stemmed shrubs. This is especially true in the glades between the tributaries of the coastal rivers. Temperatures always fall lowest in the dry Everglades, are slightly higher in the pinelands, and often in the dense tropical hammocks the drop is so slight that the vegetation is unaffected.

Some of the more important freezes of the past are of interest from the standpoints of frequency and effects. The severe freezes of 1894 and 1895 were reported in many places. They practically wiped out the citrus industry, which did not recover for some years afterward. The crop of 1896 was reduced by over 90 percent according to the *Miami Herald*. Little else is known about the effects of this freeze at the southern tip of Florida, as few settlers were present and agriculture was barely getting under way.

Another destructive freeze occurred in 1899. It was reported as being very severe at Flamingo and Cape Sable. Many full grown mahoganies were reported killed. William J. Krome, the construction engineer for the Key West

Frost on the coastal prairie. *Frosts occur somewhere in the area nearly every other year. Only severe freezes such as those of 1894-1895 and 1917 cause much damage to native vegetation. In 1895 mahoganies were reported killed at Flamingo, and extended deadenings in second-growth mangrove stands about that time suggest a similar fate. The major effect of frost is the girdling at ground line that results in the top killing of the sensitive samplings. This alters the stand composition, removing these susceptible species, and restricts their northern advance into the central portion of the area. Several types of dwarf communities are the result of frost, such as manchineel, white mangrove, buttonwood, coco plum, and poisonwood. This photograph was taken in a coastal prairie area near Flamingo where the invading buttonwoods were killed at the ground line.*

Extension of the Florida East Coast Railway, stated in a letter that he saw the dead trees in 1902 and was told by residents that the freeze of 1899 was the cause of their death. Mr. Krome was much interested in agriculture and kept records on killing frosts over a number of years. His notes, shown to me by Mrs. Krome, recorded freezes in the Homestead vicinity in January 1905, December 1906, February 1909, and March 1915.

In 1917 the worst frost on record occurred in Miami on February 3. A low of 27 degrees was reported there, while Homestead recorded 22 to 24 degrees F. This freeze killed many trees in the Miami area, particularly many large Australian pines 2 feet in diameter and 75 to 100 feet tall. The writer had occasion to examine a number of these trees in the late summer of that year at the request of local authorities at Palm Beach, who thought that an insect might be responsible for the extensive kill. The insect they suspected proved to be one of the flat-headed borers (*Chrysobotheris* sp.). This beetle lives in the inner bark of dying and dead trees and is not a primary pest. At that time it was concluded that the delayed death of the Australian pines was from the effects of the freeze. On January 4, 1918, Mr. Krome reported 24 degrees F. in Homestead. This freeze extended far into the southern glades but did little damage in Miami.

The writer has lived since 1950 in the Homestead area, and has observed and recorded data about frost injury to trees. A freeze in January 1956 was observed from the air on February 10 of that year. Considerable buttonwood was badly damaged in the eastern portions of the Park, particularly in the tree islands at the north end of Taylor River. On December 18, 1956, many buttonwoods were found top-killed around Flamingo from the January freeze. The frost of February 5, 1958, did considerable damage in the Flamingo area of the Park. In February of 1959 many dead white mangroves, manchineels, colubrina, and Jamaica

Frost in Flamingo area. *A severe freeze in January 1956 in the Flamingo area killed a second-growth stand of white mangroves. These sprouted and were again killed in December 1962. These were once again sprouting in January 1963 when this photograph was taken.*

dogwoods were observed along the Crocodile Point road. Manchineel seemed to be most seriously damaged.

In 1962 freezes occurred on December 11, 12, 13, and 14 and caused the most extensive damage since 1917. Citrus trees and avocados were badly damaged over much of South Florida. On January 2, 1963, patches of dead white mangroves were examined along the Crocodile Point road. These were top-killed by this freeze. These were sprouts from the same trees that had had their tops destroyed in the 1956 and 1958 freezes. A month later in 1963 these white mangroves were again sprouting at their bases. In the glades nearby, many buttonwoods were dead. This is suggestive of the so-called "frost pockets" of the Appalachian valleys that effectively limit tree size and distribution. In September 1963, near Punta Gorda, basal sprouts 12 to 24 inches long from white mangroves were examined on trees top-killed by the 1962 freeze. The red mangroves did not appear to be injured.

In 1964 a freeze on January 14 centered around the western part of the Park. It did much damage in the vicinity of Lostman's River and Flamingo. In 1965 a freeze occurred on January 17-18 that caused sporadic damage. On February 1 of the same year a freeze occurred over much of the Park. While flying over the area a month later, much browning of white mangrove was observed south of Joe River, north of West Lake, and in other various places in the freshwater mangrove region. It is obvious that these freezes are effective in preventing the gradual invasion of more susceptible trees into the glades.

A freeze occurred in January 1966, and another on February 1 badly damaged buttonwood and coco plum north of the rock reef that crosses the Park at Payhayokee Tower. South of this rock reef there was 0.2 to 0.5 feet of water on the surface, and no damage occurred. On March 2, 1968, there was a recorded low of 29 degrees F. at Homestead. Some scouting along the main road showed ficus, morinda, dalbergia, and trema had suffered scattered damage as far south as Snake Bight Road.

Throughout the Park the species most seriously damaged in the freezes observed by the writer are, in approximate order of their injury: manchineel, guava, trema, coco plum, buttonwood, figs, poisonwood, white mangrove, gumbo-limbo, Brazilian holly, marlberry, and red mangrove.

Lightning

Lightning strikes, the accompaniment of the frequent thunderstorms of the region, are common. Aside from the occasional fires thus started, they are of little significance. Strikes in the mangrove forest, however, often kill all of the trees within a roughly circular area of from 0.1 acre to nearly 0.5 acre. These kills had been observed many times before a recent strike was witnessed and an explanation became evident. It appears that these closely spaced trees have intermingled and grafted networks of roots. The wet peaty soil provides good conduction for carrying the lightning.

These areas are quickly repopulated by seeds of shrubs stored in the leaf litter and by the following seed crop. But usually a somewhat different proportion of species emerges, and red mangrove often predominates. This phenomenon may account in part for the irregular species mixture and

Lightning damage. *Summer thunderstorms are frequent in this area. The accompanying lightning strikes are numerous and start fires that maintain or destroy, as the case may be, certain plant communities. In the Saline Mangrove Zone circular patches of trees, one-tenth of an acre or so in area, are often killed by a single bolt. Possibly, the moist, peaty soil or root grafts carry the electricity through a number of trees. This strike occurred in Rookery Bay, Collier County, in the spring of 1967.*

mixed age classes so characteristic of the mangrove forests. A dozen such strikes were observed following a storm around Rookery Bay near Naples in the fall of 1966.

Alligators

The alligator plays a very definite role in the shaping of plant communities. This may seem an overstatement inasmuch as this reptile is listed by the U.S. Department of the Interior as an endangered species. Before white man appeared in the area, alligators were extremely abundant and dominated the entire area wherever fresh water was present, much as the buffalo dominated the prairies at one time. Gator holes were maintained in practically all plant associations, including the pinelands.

The preferred habitats of the alligator in former times were the freshwater marshes just inside the mangrove zone and the small freshwater creeks fingering into these glades. These freshwater swamps are about equally land and water, and here the alligator was dominant for at least 1,000 years. Alligators moved about in the ponds, preventing them from silting and closing over with emergent aquatic plants by actually moving materials with their snouts and tails

Gator holes. *Nearly all creeks end in gator holes. First the alligators pushed a narrow trail through the saw grass to a gator hole. These paths eventually widened and deepened into creeks. The mud eroded to bedrock and the banks became colonized by red mangroves and swamp hardwoods.*

Freshwater creeks and alligators. *In the freshwater swamp just landward to the Buttonwood Levee, the saw grass marshes form a continuous band around the tip of Florida. Here the estuaries break up into small creeks and finger several miles inland through the saw grass marshes. These swamps have been perpetuated by frequent fires that killed the ever-encroaching red mangroves and other swamp trees. They also provided the nesting sites of the once-abundant alligators, which fed nearby and sun-basked on the banks of these creeks. The alligator trails cutting through the saw grass serve as channels to permit flooding of the area with fresh water and as passageways for small animal life to move in and out with the varying water levels. The reptiles built their nests in the saw grass just off their trails, and the nests were used year after year.*

(McIlhenny, 1935; Craighead, 1968). The pools and small creeks were thus kept relatively clean while they were occupied by the reptiles. The alligators also moved from pond to pond and from creek to creek across the glades. Their trails were kept open by their tearing loose the outreaching red mangrove prop roots, thus preventing rapid closure.

Many of the mangrove creeks fingering into the freshwater zone from the main estuaries have closed in the past twenty years; this has been accelerated by the recent

Freshwater creek invaded by mangroves and hardwoods. *This freshwater creek lies downstream about two miles from the previous illustration, and shows the extensive invasion of red and white mangroves and swamp hardwoods into the saw grass swamp. This has occurred over much of the area during the past twenty years in the absence of fires and the decrease in alligators.*

curtailed flow of water and the decline in numbers of alligators. The red mangrove prop roots reach out from the bank and finally meet, debris accumulates, and in time the flow of water is checked. Many such creeks are now visible from the air as buttonwood strands fringed with red mangroves. Some of these, now closed, in the watersheds of the North and Roberts rivers were passable with canoe in the early fifties.

Alligator nests are constructed of plant materials heaped up 2 to 3 feet high and 6 to 8 feet wide, with increments added year after year as the basal vegetation compacts. They form innumerable small hummocks in the saw grass marshes bordering the many freshwater creeks or on the rims of the

Alligator hummock in saw grass. *Since the alligator has been decimated many nesting sites such as the one illustrated are no longer used. Fern spores blow in, floating seeds drift in, and berry stones are dropped by resting birds. From the replacement vegetation, some buttonwood islands and small bay heads emerge that slowly enlarge in a circular pattern.*

gator holes. When abandoned by the alligators, they become colonized by buttonwood, red bay, myrtle, leather ferns, and swamp ferns. These plants signaled the beginning of the end of many saw grass marshes as the general water table lowered.

Bay heads were also desirable nesting sites. Here repeated nesting has perceptibly raised the maximum elevations 1 to

Alligator hummock. *The alligator once dominated the freshwater creeks and the solution holes in the pineland, and large males entered the mangrove flats during the rainy seasons. Along the creek banks and beyond in the saw grass, nests were constructed by piling and compacting vegetation. These small mounds were enlarged each year, gradually forming hard masses of peat that were resistant to decay and fire. This hummock was formed in a former saw grass community that was later inundated by the rising sea; then the saw grass was replaced by juncus. Some years later red mangroves began to invade, but some plants of both species still remain. This hummock may be as much as 500 years of age.*

3 feet. Alligators also require caves where they can retreat in cool weather or when disturbed. Many natural caves are available in the eroded bedrock, and others are dug into banks under supporting tree roots. The alligators pile plant material over their caves to a height of about 2 feet, and this material supports shrubby growth (Craighead, 1968).

2 ❧ Geology and Physiography

The geology of the area is relatively simple, and for the most part the surficial soils are of Recent age. Limestone formations outcrop or shallowly underlie the mainland soils over most of the region and give an alkaline character to the soil. To the east an outcropping coastal ridge of Miami oolite forms the eastern boundary of the great Everglades swamp. This is a Pleistocene limestone. The roughly eroded, outcropping adjacent limestone west and beneath this ridge has recently been described by J. E. Hoffmeister et al. (1967) as a Bryozoan limestone. The heavily arenaceous (sandy) limestone outcropping over most of western Monroe and Collier counties is known as the Tamiami formation and is of Miocene age. At places these sands are deep, and the soil tends to be acid. A fine deposit of quartz sand throughout the headwater sloughs of the Rodgers, Broad, and Lostman's rivers on the west coast and the north coastal ridge in Dade County is assigned to the Anastasia formation. The upper Keys are a coral rock formation of the Pleistocene age. The lower Keys are an extension of the Miami oolitic limestone.

Most of the soil over the area—that is, the overburden on the shallow bedrock and in the numerous solution holes and mudbanks of the Florida Bay keys—is of Recent origin, less than 5,000 years of age. These soils are almost entirely calcareous muds and peats precipitated or deposited by plants and mixed with remains of shell. They have been formed in quiet waters contemporaneous with the rising sea or in impounded fresh water. They vary from a few inches

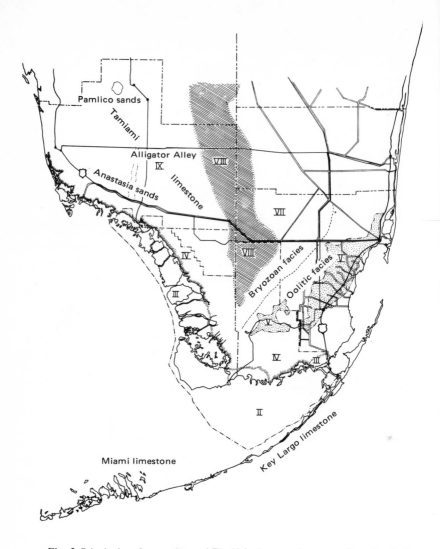

Fig. 3. Principal surface geology of Florida's three southern counties; after Puri
and Vernon (1964) and Hoffmeister et al. (1967).
Miami limestone (Pleistocene)
    Oolitic facies
    Bryozoan facies
Tamiami limestone (Miocene), partly covered by
    Anastasia Sands (Pleistocene)
    Pamlico Sands
Key Largo limestone (Pleistocene)

to over 6 feet in depth, at places in the Ten Thousand Islands reaching 14 feet or more. The sandy soils have been derived from disintegration of the bedrock or have been deposited by ocean currents. More detailed information has been given by Parker, Ferguson, and Love (1955), Puri and Vernon (1964), and Hoffmeister et al. (1967).

The physiography of the area is of great consequence to the plants growing here. This is an uncommonly flat land. The highest elevation, the rocky ridge along the eastern coast, varies from about 20 feet in North Miami to about 2 feet at its southern end at Mahogany Hammock in Everglades National Park. Some 40 miles to the west the Tamiami limestone rises 7 to 13 feet. Between these ridges lies the great Everglades marsh. This marsh slopes gradually south and west to the coast. All of these formations are pitted with solution holes, shallow basins, or cut with deeper sloughs that formerly formed the beds of shallow streams. Geologists attribute this karst surface to erosion, caused by the water sinking through the porous rock many years ago when the sea was 25 to 50 feet lower than at present. These minor features control the distribution of the vegetation today. The solution holes, basins, and sloughs hold moisture and collect peat on which the swamp plants grow. The higher elevations and rocky outcrops that are frequently scarred by fires support the pine forests and tropical hardwood hammocks. Around the tip of the mainland the bedrock is 6 to 15 feet deep. On this lies a great crescent-shaped area of deep organic soil that is washed by the daily tides and forested by mangroves.

The adjustments of many of the plants to this terrain and how some have helped to shape it are described in more detail in later pages.

The Rising Sea

The extensive deposits of marl, shell, and peat up to 12 feet or more in thickness that form the recently deposited land surrounding the tip of Florida have been preserved by the slowly rising sea of the past 5,000 years. John H. Davis, Jr. (1940), in reporting on his extensive studies of the mangroves of southern Florida, pointed out that the

Coastal or Flamingo embankment. *The coastal or Flamingo embankment 2 miles north of Flamingo near Cactus Point is shown in this photograph. Here it is composed of a narrow marl shoreline carrying scattered large black mangroves; a strip of coastal prairie with batis; and to the rear a mangrove flat at mean sea level. The dead stubs are remains of mangroves destroyed in 1935. Behind the dead trees is a narrow margin of living mangroves. To the rear are patches of mangroves, shallow ponds, and buttonwood strands, which continue north to Bear Lake. The higher ground here is 1.5 feet msl and the lowest a few tenths above or below sea level.*

deep peat beds of these swamps indicate a recent rise in sea level of at least 7 feet. More extensive information has been summarized recently by D. W. Scholl and Minze Stuvier (1967, 1969). Their studies show a total rise of approximately four meters (about 12 feet), equivalent to about 3 inches per each 100 years.

As the water rose with intermittant halts, several shorelines were formed on the limestone bedrock. On this emergent soil, vegetation was quickly established, trapping more debris, mud, shell, and sand and thus gradually increasing the elevation by 1 to 3 feet, and even to 6 feet on beaches where shell was abundant. In the quiet lagoons behind the coastal embankments, mangroves and other

Cape Sable beaches. *East Cape Sable is illustrated here to show the sand-shell beach on a marl subsoil. Alternating low dunes and troughs and a tropical hardwood hammock are to the rear. Behind the hammock strand lies a batis flat with herbaceous halophytes and a large area of mangrove flats that extends out to Ingraham Lake. Each severe storm changes the beach outline; in the past few years the three capes have been extending and the bays eroding. The low swale between the dunes carry contrasting vegetation to that of the slightly higher (12-24 in.) dunes. A reservoir of fresh water held in these dunes was extensively utilized in the days of sailing ships, which depended on such sites for obtaining supplies of fresh water.*

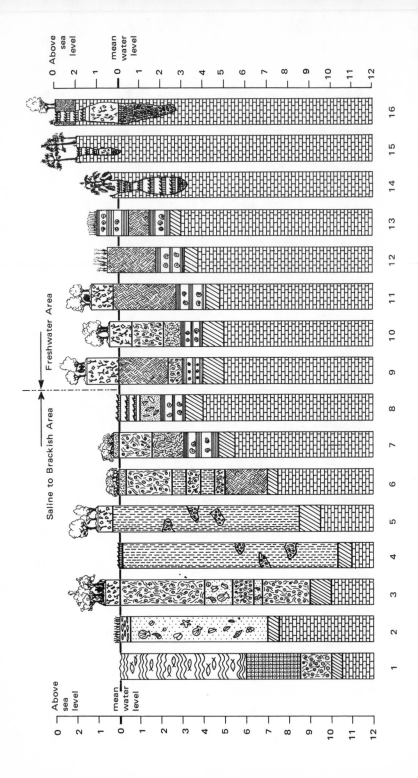

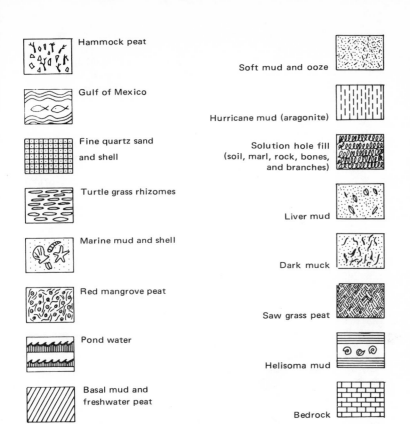

Hammock peat

Gulf of Mexico

Fine quartz sand
and shell

Turtle grass rhizomes

Marine mud and shell

Red mangrove peat

Pond water

Basal mud and
freshwater peat

Soft mud and ooze

Hurricane mud (aragonite)

Solution hole fill
(soil, marl, rock, bones,
and branches)

Liver mud

Dark muck

Saw grass peat

Helisoma mud

Bedrock

Fig. 4. Stratigraphy of Recent Sediments From the Gulf of Mexico Off Broad
River and Florida Bay Mudbanks to the Pinelands of Dade County

*Each column represents the profile of the sediments from the surface of the
water, soil or rock into the limestone bedrock. The oldest sediments, found lying on the bedrock under Man O' War Key in Florida Bay, are 5,300 years old.*

1. Gulf of Mexico. *Red Mangrove peat representing the site of a mangrove
forest 5,000 years ago, now covered with sand and shell and the rising sea.*

2. Florida Bay Mud Flats. *These muds are built up on freshwater peat by the
precipitation of calcitic materials from plants, and also contain shells and
animal remains. A variety of plants form the living community at or just below
mean sea level.*

3. Murray Key. *The perimeter of the island is composed of tough mangrove
peat that protects the island from storm tides.*

4. Murray Key. *Interior of the same island which has been filled with
hurricane mud.*

5. Flamingo Embankment. *Storm and tidal action have deposited sediments
in the vegetation to form a levee of higher ground along the coast of Florida Bay.*

6. Mangrove Flat. *In this community, deep deposits of peat and marl have
collected in the quiet waters behind the Flamingo Levee.* Continued on p. 40.

7. River Bank. *Slight embankments also form along the estuaries and fresh-water creeks.*

8. Ponds, Lakes, and Bays. *As the quiet waters behind the coastal and river embankments fill with peat and marl, ponds, lakes, and bays of various depths and sizes remain. These gradually close as the sediments accumulate.*

9. Buttonwood Embankment. *Along the landward edge of the Saline Man-grove Zone the Buttonwood Embankment has formed. This impounds the freshwater swamps of the three-county area.*

10. Upper River Banks. *The upper freshwater tributaries likewise form embankments that gradually change from a mangrove flora to that of freshwater swamp and finally to saw grass as they finger into the freshwater marshes.*

11. Bayheads. *In the freshwater marshes tree islands of the bay head type are common. These build up on a mass of hammock peat, sometimes as much as 3 feet above the normal water level.*

12. Saw Grass Marshes. *The saw grass marshes have occupied essentially the same position for at least 3,000 years. Characteristic peat beds have built up. As the sea gradually rises, so do these freshwater marshes. Red and white mangroves invade across the Buttonwood Embankment and in the absence of fire gradually replace the saw grass for as much as 15 miles inland.*

13. Spike Rush Marshes. *These communities form a considerable part of the freshwater marshes. They occur chiefly on shallow marl soil where the bedrock is near the surface.*

14. Willow Heads and Cypress Domes. *These tree islands spot the freshwater marshes beyond the reach of hurricane tides. They usually develop around depressions in the bedrock.*

15. Pineland. *The rock lands of the Miami limestone ridge are characterized by stands of pine and numerous solution holes and hammocks.*

16. Tropical Hardwood Hammocks. *Hammock vegetation is composed of many tropical hardwoods and a few species from the temperate zone. A layer of hammock peat builds up beneath this vegetation.*

Red mangrove prop roots. *Red mangrove forms deep layers of peat where the plants grow in protected waters, such as along estuaries and on mangrove flats. These prop roots begin to form in the third year of seedling growth. They push down through 3 to 4 feet of mud, rarely more. The marl is completely replaced by prop roots, which die after a few years, leaving a long column of peat. These columns gradually coalesce to form the peat beds underneath the trees. The presence of living roots in deeper peat has confused carbon dating results.*

brackish water plants flourished, forming beds of peat several feet in thickness on top of the marl beds deposited by plants and hurricanes.

It would appear that the greatest inland extension of a marine shoreline during this period may have closely paralleled the present embankments along the landward edge of the saline mangrove swamps. Named the Buttonwood Embankment, or Buttonwood Levee (Craighead, 1964), it runs approximately along the north shore of the chain of lakes and bays that cross the tip of Florida. At places on the bedrock, marine shell beaches covered by several strata of hurricane mud, peat, and mud-bearing freshwater shells are found. This beachline of shell, peat, and marl follows approximately the 5 foot depth of bedrock, at least east of the Lostman's River area. Seaward, the bedrock drops rapidly to 7 to 13 feet below mean sea level, and landward rises gradually and outcrops from one-half to 10 miles inland.

The present shoreline, one-half to 10 miles seaward, forms the north shore of Florida Bay to Cape Sable, and hence north to form the shore of the Gulf of Mexico. This shoreline, called the Flamingo Embankment, is chiefly marine marl deposited by hurricanes. North of Cape Sable it is composed of a mixture of shell and quartz sand. The Buttonwood and Flamingo embankments separate the freshwater and saline swamps, respectively. Between them lie several temporary shorelines that support tropical hardwoods.

The seaward-sloping, eroded bedrock of Florida Bay that was exposed 5,000 years ago, to all indications, appears similar to that now outcropping 2 to 15 miles inland. Tree islands, buttonwood strands, and sloughs were once present and had similar vegetation. Many of the keys in Florida Bay were then represented by bay heads growing in depressions of the bedrock. They were surrounded by a perimeter of red mangroves growing in shallow fresh water, exactly what we now have several miles inland in the freshwater swamps. As the sea rose, a solid perimeter of firm mangrove peat, which is very resistant to decay and erosion, was preserved. The dense tangle of prop roots collected organic debris and

Pitted marl surface. *Hurricane Donna tore off large blocks of peat together with the mangroves to leave this much-pitted marl surface. This marl bed, which is stratified with shell and sand and lenses of peat, is 2 to 11 feet deep. A later storm completely covered this marl with sand and shell that extended several hundred feet into the living mangroves shown at the rear. Some blocks of peat held together by the red mangrove roots were floated far inland.*

calcareous mud and built up a rich soil 50 to 100 feet behind the shoreline. This became colonized by several species of shrubs, grasses, and sedges and finally by buttonwood and other tropical hardwoods. At the same time the interiors of these keys were filled with fine-grained sediments formed on the adjacent mudbanks and transported across the atoll-like rim by storms. These periodic mud invasions destroyed the plants established in the interior, maintaining an open flat or pond seasonally brackish or saline. As the rising salt water gradually overran the freshwater swamps, extensive surrounding mudbanks were formed from the deposits of marine plants and animals. The vertical growth of these flats likewise kept pace with the rising sea under the protection of marine plants, chiefly turtle grass and various algae. A great part of the fill of these mudbanks is derived from mollusks and the detritus of foraminifera and calcareous algae. These mud flats are quite uniform down to bedrock; they are composed of calcareous silt and shell, with only an occasional lens of mangrove peat. Bedrock here is usually shallower than under the Florida Bay keys (Craighead, 1969).

The character of the surface soil, marl or shell beaches, and inland peat or marl deposits, and their elevation in relation to tidal overflow, governs the present vegetation— strand plants along the coast, tropical hardwoods on the higher coastal elevations and shell mounds, mangroves on the tidal flats, and buttonwood hammocks on the inter- mediate elevations that are subject to occasional tidal overflow.

Detail of prop roots in marl. *This enlargement shows those prop roots remaining after the mangroves had been torn away.*

Big Sable Creek. *The delta of Big Sable Creek is gradually moving inland as degradation proceeds with the slowly rising sea. This process is still farther advanced just north at the mouth of the Shark River. Red mangrove peat beds lie under 10 feet of water a mile offshore, marking the site of former forests. The pattern of erosion shown here is (1) the mangroves are killed by deposits of hurricane mud; (2) storm tides gradually eat out the unconsolidated peat and soft mud; (3) the trees topple and are carried out to sea by the hurricane backwash. On each outgoing tide, quantities of the loosened and finely to coarsely divided organic matter color the flow and often form longshore deposits along the beaches farther south.*

Receding beach at Big Sable Creek. *This beach just south of Big Sable Creek is now receding after a period of upbuilding. A stratum of peat from Big Sable Creek is exposed after it had been buried by a deposit of shell and sand.*

Cape Sable beach. *Beaches around the tip of Florida come and go. They may be composed of quartz sand, shell, marl, seaweed, or mangroves. Each hurricane or severe storm has its effect. Some build beaches of shell or sand; others leave a shoreline packed with seaweed or a stand of mangroves just inshore from where a beach existed a few days before. But when undisturbed for several years, red mangrove creeps slowly outward if the water is shallow and the prop roots can reach the mud within 18 to 24 inches. Here the rising sea is undoing what past hurricanes constructed. This portion of the beautiful sandy beach is being slowly inundated; first the sand and shell beach, then the prairie, and now the tropical hammock. All of these communities have been submerged and carried away in succession. At other places around the tip of Florida several forms of shorelines are found. All are transient, geologically speaking, here for a day and then gone forever.*

Landward of the saline mangrove swamps behind the Buttonwood Embankment extending across the area are the impounded freshwater swamps of marl and peat, bearing the freshwater plant associations such as saw grass and spike rush swamps and buttonwood strands, bay heads, willow heads, and cypress domes. Still farther inland are the limestone outcrops of pine and hammock growth. All of these associations except those on the limestone outcrops are indirectly supported by the rising sea. In these impounded waters the periphyton precipitate the marls, and the peats gradually build up under the saw grass, cypress, willows, and swamp hardwoods.

Topography, Drainage, and Vegetation

In a land of such low relief, much of which is sometimes dry and at other times wet, the vegetation types express physical features, which in turn mark the drainage pattern. All three are intimately associated and are expressive of one another. The close relationship between elevation, water, and vegetation in this area has long been recognized. A difference of two inches in the average water level for a short time at a given place results in profound changes in the vegetation. This is well illustrated along the Flamingo road where, on the sloping berm, high land grasses, shrubs, and trees grow vigorously a few inches from the glade plants. In many places a wall of trees has developed on this berm in the past ten years that completely shuts off the view. Glade buggy tracks of forty years ago are still visible as two wheel ruts of contrasting vegetation. Even the mangroves that have some roots anchored in the well-aerated road berm grow much more rapidly than the adjacent swamp trees.

Lamar Johnson in 1958 aptly expressed the importance of water: "Water is the basis of being of the Everglades National Park—past, present, and future. The total bionomics of the Park are the result of the influences of water. The unique flora was fostered largely by a water environment." After discussing the future demands for water in the Central and Southern Florida Flood Control District, he concluded that "one drop of water must now preserve what two drops of water created." This is certainly true today for the true swamps of the region. But when the high lands are considered, those that depend entirely on rainfall, a somewhat different situation exists. In other words, the water needs of the Park are normally met by the average rainfall patterns. Only the true marshlands need excess water flowing from the north, and then only when drought conditions are serious.

The source of water in this three-county area in historic times seems to have been chiefly rainfall plus the flow from adjacent higher lands to the immediate north. There is little evidence to show that water of any consequence came to the Park from Lake Okeechobee, as is often stated. Some water spilled over the south shore in 1912, 1922, 1924, and 1926, according to Johnson (1958). The levee along the south shore completed in 1926 was breached by a hurricane that year and again in 1928; the later case resulted in a tragic loss of lives. It would take an exceptional head of water to push through 100 miles of saw grass to reach the Park before it all disappeared from evapotranspiration. The waters from Lake Okeechobee, even if they did once reach the Park, were distributed only through Shark River Slough and thus affected an area of less than one-third of Park land. This slough is now shut off by Levee 67 Extended, and the former flow from the north is supplied from Conservation Area 3 through four gates on the Tamiami Trail.

Collier County receives no water from Lake Okeechobee and, in fact, rainfall from the northeastern section flows into Conservation Area 3. In Monroe County, the Florida Keys depend entirely on rainfall. The mangrove swamps along Florida Bay and the Gulf of Mexico are largely watered by tides, summer rains, and overflow during the rainy season from the freshwater swamps behind the Buttonwood Levee.

The movement of water within Everglades National Park is still imperfectly known. Had the necessary details of the local drainage system been considered, the construction of Canal C-111 would never have been authorized, nor would the four big drainage structures supposed to lead water from Conservation Area 3 into the Park have been constructed.

How much water is available to the vegetation of the lower levels, i.e., the freshwater mangrove swamps through the Biscayne aquifer under the pineland ridge? The many springs of fresh water bubbling from the bedrock of the small tributaries of the coastal swamps suggest that this amount could be considerable.

What is the rate of flow in the Park, if any? The vegetation of this relatively flat land serves as an accurate indicator of water levels. The plants reflect differences in water levels that are maintained for several months, and the flow, when present, is indicated by the trend of the stems of submerged plants. The map (Fig. 5) based on the vegetation attempts to outline the several drainage patterns of the area.

Fig. 5. Drainage pattern of the three southern counties of Florida. *During the rainy season definite flow can be observed while the waters are high. This is most evident at the culverts along the road where the water is somewhat impounded, especially following heavy rains. As the dry season approaches, flow ceases and the water becomes impounded in the numerous irregularities of the bedrock and in the impervious sands and marls. As this proceeds many living organisms are concentrated in these ponds. This is of great biological significance and might be considered characteristic of these swamps and marshes. Practically all animal and plant life are adapted to this wet-dry climate.*

The movement of water on this flatland is often hardly perceptible. It is further slowed down by the vegetation and also may be humped by the wind. Heavy rains lie in a hump and take days to flatten. Often the water levels do not conform to that of the land.

The period of time that a given spot is wet or dry is the important factor, not how much water passes over that spot.

Southern Florida south of Lake Okeechobee is a remarkably flat country. Elevations at the northern end of the Everglades are around 17 feet. From here, there is a gradual slope to sea level at the mouth of the Shark River some 100 miles south. This is a gradient of less than 0.2 foot per mile.

Several maps showing the drainage systems within the Park have been published, but these depict only the high water level drainage patterns. Actually, there are two distinct drainage patterns—one of flood waters and one of impounded waters. The former operates during the average rainy season and locally when the water "humps" from scattered, heavy precipitation. The latter is operative after the excess runs off over the Buttonwood Embankment at about 1.2 to 1.5 feet just inland from this levee. In some years this flow lasted throughout the dry season.

The impounded waters are most important, biologically speaking. They slowly evaporate or are gradually lost by transpiration through the leaves of the plants that they support. At present there is no accurate contour map of the area to outline these low basins and sloughs that hold impounded water.

There are three rocky outcrops extending in a northeast-southwesterly direction that divide any flow of fresh water from the north into the three main sloughs or drainages. These are not of sufficient elevation to be readily recognized by sight, but the vegetation is distinctive and an actual observable flow may be visible after heavy rains that form a local water hump.

The most eastern high land is the Miami oolite that outcrops from North Miami through Homestead and extends as a curving ridge southwest to Mahogany Hammock. Elevations on this ridge are greatest around Miami (20 feet) and gradually fall to about 7 feet at the Park entrance and to 2 feet at Mahogany Hammock. This ridge is broken by several shallow sloughs that drain east or southeast into Biscayne Bay. At present these carry water only when very high, humped waters such as those accompanying hurricanes occur (Hartwell, 1968).

The Miami ridge gradually tapers in a westerly slope toward the Shark River Slough. Much of this slope is a rough, rocky country of pinnacle rock with islands of pine or hammock growth and numerous ponds and small sloughs intermixed. This rocky area forms the eastern bank of the Shark River Slough, and is crossable by airboat only at a few places and only at maximum water levels. The central part of this limestone drains toward the slough from Grossman Hammock to form Taylor Slough. Much of this water comes from the pineland to the east, land now largely in farm crops. This drainage breaks through the Miami Ridge at Long Pine Key near the Park entrance and extends on to Little Madeira Bay as an intermittant river now well filled with bay heads and peaty soils. Early Homestead residents report using this watercourse to skiff out to Florida Bay around 1900.

The third height of land extends north and south of Forty Mile Bend. North of the Tamiami Trail it forms the western boundary of the great Everglades swamp. It averages about 7 feet above mean sea level in the Park and as high as 10 to 13 feet north of the Trail. Three of the four gates from Conservation Area 3 along the Trail open into this. The insufficient flow from these gates across this higher ground has necessitated the diversion of water into Canal 67 Extended and then into the Shark River Slough. This higher ground west of the Shark River Slough is an area of rocky hammock outcrops with numerous saw grass and spike rush sloughs between. There is much scrub cypress in these sloughs where impounded water remains for much of the year. The vegetation of the many tropical hardwood hammocks is characteristic of higher land that held little standing water in the past.

West of this ridge lies the Big Cypress Swamp. The drainage here at high water is south and west through numerous sloughs, cypress strands, and culverts under the Tamiami Trail. At lower levels the water is impounded into numerous ponds.

Cypress is short and scrubby where the soil is thin but is of excellent growth in the sloughs. Many large tropical hardwood hammocks or patches of pine are features of the highest outcrops. The vegetation of this area was seriously damaged by the fires of 1962 and 1965. In the western portion of the Big Cypress the sloughs are larger, deeper, and in the recent past were forested with excellent cypress stands. Many have now been logged and burned.

Within the Park the great body of freshwater swamps just inland to the Saline Mangrove Zone and farther inland appear to lack any water flow after the excess runs off. Here the water is controlled by an intricate series of basins rising from zero to 5 feet in elevation near the Trail. The full import of the biological needs and management of water in the Park will not be fully understood until these basins and embankments are mapped and the extent of the resultant impounding thoroughly investigated.

In the freshwater zone, embankments are formed by the rock reefs, irregularities of the bedrock, and from the marl banks precipitated by the periphyton and peat from swamp trees. These offer little obstruction to the high water runoff into the tidal swamps of the Park, nor do they form an entirely complete system of blockage for the impounded fresh water inasmuch as they are more or less broken and overlapping. Lamar Johnson (1958) realized the significance of these embankments and suggested that a roadway be constructed across the Park between the saline and freshwater zones for fire protection purposes and as a means of slowing down freshwater runoff by repairing gaps. Such construction would not be consistent with generally accepted Park Service policy; however, if a practical means of repair of those portions of the Buttonwood Embankment destroyed by fire in the past fifty years could be devised, the runoff period could be lengthened.

Although the pattern of all of these impoundments and embankments is incompletely known, several have been studied in some detail. The most important is the Buttonwood Embankment extending across the Park along the landward edge of the Saline Mangrove Zone. This levee separates normal tidal waters from the impounded fresh water.

Beginning at US 1 and Canal C-111 in the southeastern corner of the Park, there is a low (1.5 feet msl, or mean sea

Detail of the north shore of West Lake. *This enlargement shows the Buttonwood Embankment, the band of saw grass, and the two small creeks crossing this community.*

level) marl levee extending to near Little Madeira Bay. Here it lies inland nearly 1 mile from Florida Bay. It is forested with numerous buttonwood tree islands. From Little Madeira Bay to the Flamingo road there is an effective bank 1.5 to 2 feet in elevation, with only three minor creeks cutting through. This levee lies on the north shore of Little and Big Madeira bays, Seven Palm Lake, and Cuthbert, Long, and West lakes. Over most of this distance, the impounding of water north of the embankment has resulted in the deposition of peat one-half to 5 miles inland to Nine Mile Pond and northeast along Madeira Slough; the latter is locally called the Big Thicket.

West of the Flamingo road from West Lake across the East, Rodgers, North, and Watson rivers, the Buttonwood Embankment now follows the banks of the tributaries that finger into the freshwater swamps. It is broken at many places by fires of the past fifty years, and salt water now pushes as far inland as Mahogany Hammock when strong southwest winds coincide with the absence of a freshwater buffer in the Everglades.

Across the Shark River drainage to the Rodgers River, the impounded water lies almost entirely behind the elevated creek banks. Farther inland, however, about 1 mile north of the U.S. Geological Survey gauging station P-35, is a broad, low embankment of marl and peat about 1 foot higher than the general ground level.

West from the Rodgers across the several rivers to Everglades City, a low, well defined embankment lies along the north shore of the string of lakes and bays and outward along the banks of the many small creeks that finger into the glades and enter these ponds. The many rock reefs in the Park also form a series of water impounding embankments.

Solution Holes

Among the most interesting features of South Florida are the many solution holes in the soft limestone and bedrock. In the higher rock land hammocks, solution holes are numerous and are usually well developed. Many are 10 feet deep, and some are as much as 20, and from 1 to 30 feet in width. The openings are usually of a smaller diameter than the well portion, which usually widens in a dumbbell shape. These holes were formed when the sea was much lower by waters charged with carbonic acids that slowly percolated through the porous limestone. Some are still open, but most have become plugged with marl and hold water during the rainy season. It would be of interest to determine if these holes are still enlarging under the action of the plant inhabitants. A suggestion of current deepening is supported by the several inches of soft, soapy, decomposed limestone at the extreme bottom of many of these solution holes.

In the hammocks and higher pineland the solution holes may be open to near the bottom, or filled with sand or a peaty soil with some darkly stained marl and peat at the bottom. In the Everglades, marl is usually predominant and fills the holes except for those occupied by plants. In these, the marl has been dissolved and replaced with peat. Fire is an important agent in the removal of this peat. When dry it burns slowly, often until it is all consumed or until the fire reaches the water table. Profiles from glades solution holes

Solution holes. *Solution holes, sinks, or potholes, as they are variously termed, are characteristic of much of this limestone area. In the pineland the holes are often deep, 15 to 20 feet, and are usually larger below ground. Others are shallow basins formed by underground solutions that cause the collapse of the surface rock. Many are cave-like and interconnected. They may be partly filled with marl, sand, or peat, and they carry many types of vegetation. Bones of extinct mammals have been found in one of the deeper solution holes near Homestead.*

often show several strata of alternating peat and marl reflecting changing water conditions.

A great variety of plant communities occupies these solution holes, and their growth and replacement is a most intriguing subject for study. Most of the holes retain water quite well and consequently support marsh plants. Quite often pure stands of plants occur; these are usually in those holes with a diameter of from 2 to 3 feet. In the still larger holes many species may be found. Many holes are found completely filled with trees—willow, pond apple, wax myrtle, dahoon holly, red bay, sweet bay, and coco plum. Some holes are occupied with one species exclusively; these may be liverworts, swamp ferns, leather ferns, arrowleaf, pickerelweed, bitter cress, water purslane, mermaid weed, spilanthes, maiden cane, black panicum, reed, saw grass, cord grass, primrose willow, water pennywort, frog's-bit, hemp vine, marsh fleabane, goldenrod, knotweed, everglade daisy, thoroughwort, dolls daisy, aster, or hibiscus.

Rock Reefs

When flying low over the Shark River Slough or the glades to the east, one's attention is attracted to long ribbons of trees spanning the open glades and connecting a series of tree islands. On closer inspection these are seen to be long, narrow rock ridges, known in provincial terminology as "rock reefs" or "hogbacks." They rise abruptly 2 to 5 feet out of the surrounding marl floor. The surface may be almost intact, resembling a paved highway, but usually it is pitted with many holes. At other places where erosion has been active from beneath, the reef is reduced to a series of inverted cones supporting the harder exposed surface.

These rock reefs may extend for many miles in fairly straight lines or they may be broadly curved or, rarely, intersect one another. They may be broken by erosion into

Rock reefs. *Long, narrow ridges of rock abruptly projecting 2 to 4 feet above the glades are a characteristic feature of the glade lands. Often these reefs are broken by erosion, and form a string of islands. Frequently they are covered with hammock trees. They appear to be shorelines of shallow seas where the rock surface has become indurated and resistant to erosion. The land surface is frequently higher by 6 to 18 inches on the upstream side of these low "hogbacks." They often define contrasting plant communities.*

a series of islands, as is now the case of those that cross the Shark River Slough. They apparently are characteristic of the Bryozoan limestone.

In the mangrove country most of the reefs have been broken down and covered with 2 feet or more of mud and peat. Remnants of such reefs have been encountered when probing for soil samples, and occasionally portions remain in the upper reaches of the freshwater creeks where they form an obstacle when cruising the creeks in a skiff. Whiskey Creek, now flowing through a long strand of red mangroves and buttonwoods, occupies the site of an old rock reef. Here the inverted pinnacles have all dissolved or toppled into the deepening slough that now replaces the rock reef. Gradually the slough has been filled with deposits of marl and peat 4 to 6 feet deep and is colonized by red mangroves and buttonwood. The creek itself has in places formed a new course, now on one side, then on the other, of the former rock reef. Most of this creek bank, some 10 miles long, still forms a boundary or embankment that restricts the flow of fresh water and impounds a glade land marsh to the north.

Many of the rock reefs run in a general east to west direction—in other words, across the present drainage. They usually mark an abrupt change in elevation in a glade. One that can be easily observed is crossed by the Flamingo road at the "Rock Reef" marker, about 9 miles south of Park headquarters.

A large basin locally known as Dwarf Cypress Pond, about 5 miles in diameter, lies to the south of this rock reef. The ground level is 12 to 18 inches lower than that to the north. This site reflects a distinct change of vegetation; numerous bay heads and cypress heads grow in the low, wet depression.

The better preserved rock reefs form a continuous elevated mesa that supports forests of tropical hardwood hammock trees. Downstream, patches of organic fill collect; swamp hardwoods, willows, and cypress take hold to form a triangular mass of vegetation based on the reef. These taper to points, some of them a mile downstream. They finally end in a long tail of saw grass or reed (Phragmites). The undercut reefs provide a series of deep gator holes and caves, where the alligators in turn have played their part in determining the character of this vegetation. Joe Ree Hammock, south and west of the Pahayokee Tower, is an excellent and readily approachable example of the vegetation buildup behind a rock reef. Here the gator holes are deep and, in the disastrous 1962 to 1965 droughts, provided one of the very few water refuges for pond life.

Some of the more conspicuous rock reefs in or near the Park are Grossman Hammock Reef, which extends from Grossman Hammock, situated about 10 miles south of the Tamiami Trail, in a westerly direction some 7 miles to near the eastern Park boundary just outside its northeast corner; Joe Ree Rock Reef, which extends from the Shark River Slough through the Pahayokee Tower across the Flamingo road at Culvert 34, onward over 10 miles into the pineland near Pine Glade Pond, and thence, curving, contacts the Flamingo road at the intersection of the Pineland campground and Royal Palm roads; Ficus Hammock Rock Reef, from the Shark River Slough along the north side of Ficus Hammock, across the Flamingo road at Culvert 56, and on to Atoll Hammock; the Pineland Rock Reef, which extends from Atoll Hammock northeast through the Miami pine ridge to the western end of the Farm Road; Whiskey Creek Rock Reef, previously mentioned; two Watson River rock reefs some 5 miles north of Dead-end Pond on the Watson River; several short rock reefs following along the ridge of high hammocks south of Forty Mile Bend to Ten Mile Corner; and a reef extending from near the Canepatch on Squaw Creek southeasterly for about 8 miles (this reef may originally have connected with the Ficus Rock Reef).

The origin of rock reefs has not been given much study, nor has any good description of these reefs been presented. They are an important feature of the topography of the Park and greatly influence its drainage system. They provide rock elevations supporting tropical hardwoods, and downstream they form an environment suitable for the development of bay heads and cypress forests.

Rock reefs appear to mark old shorelines of former bays, lakes, and ponds of the subsiding seas. The composition of

Fig. 6. More important rock reefs of the Everglades National Park: *(1) Grossman Hammock; (2) Joe Ree Rock Reef; (3) Ficus Hammock Rock Reef; (4) Pineland Rock Reef; (5) Whiskey Creek Rock Reef; (6) Watson River Rock Reef; (7) Squaw Creek Rock Reef; (8) West Boundary Rock Reef; and (9) Scattered remnants in the Shark River Slough.*

the basal rock appears to be that of the adjacent limestone, while the exposed surface has one to three millimeters of very dense calcite resistant to erosion. The material immediately below this surface crust is also denser than the adjacent limestone.

Wilson H. Monroe's studies (1966) of the formation of tropical karst topography in Puerto Rico by solution and reprecipitation of limestone to form an indurated capping seem to be applicable to the erosion-resistant surface of these rock reefs. The exposed limestone outcrops in our region are often coated with a blanket of blue-green algae during the rainy season. This mat of algae, often one-half inch thick, appears quickly (within three days) in moist, humid to rainy weather and may prove to be one of the plants responsible for the formation of the insoluable cap. D. W. Scholl and William H. Taft (1964) call attention to the role of algae in the formation of calcareous tufts in Mono Lake, California.

Soils and Vegetation

Foresters have long known the importance of soils in determining tree distribution and site quality. The arborescent vegetation of an area, in fact, almost invariably gives a good clue to its soil characteristics. The early colonists in the northeastern United States soon learned to choose their farm sites by indicator trees. The "walnut bottoms" with their deep, rich soil were cleared first. In this area, likewise, vegetation sharply defines soil types, modified of course by other factors such as elevation and fire.

As the first farmers moved into South Florida around seventy years ago, they found the peaty soil of the solution holes and sinks the most fertile. The first agriculture of the region was confined to the potholes in the coral rock of the Florida Keys. Many articles were written on pothole farming (Gifford, 1945-1946).

In general, the soil types fairly well coincide with the physiographic provinces of the areas next described. The agricultural soils have been well studied and described by the U.S. Soil Conservation Service and the Florida Agricultural Experiment Stations (Soil Survey, Collier County,

Coring device. *A homemade coring device used in sampling marl and peat deposits of Recent age, to about 15 feet in depth. This simple device uses a 2-inch aluminum irrigation pipe, two poles, and two 2-inch rubber stoppers. It has given excellent results; more than 500 cores have been taken in sampling various soil types in the area.*

1954; Soil Survey, Dade County, 1958). In their bulletins the soil series are named and the soil classes described. The mangrove soils forming a belt around the coastline and in Florida Bay where high salinity is a dominating characteristic have not, however, received much attention. A recent unpublished report by W. R. Llewellyn (1967) describes several types.

For the purpose of pointing out relationships between the woody plants mentioned here and the soils, the use of the broader soil series—Rocky Soils, Sandy Soils, Marl Soils, and Organic Soils—are usually sufficient.

Rocky Soils

These soils make up a considerable acreage in all three counties. The softer limestones of Dade County are being used more and more for agricultural purposes. They represent the highest and best-drained soils of the region. The numerous potholes once were rich in organic deposits and were quite fertile. Around 1950 heavy equipment was developed to break up the pitted rock surface and to mix the organic and mineral elements; this technique has made thousands of acres available for winter crops.

Several soil types have been described based on the four outcropping limestones—Miami oolite or Rockdale soil; Bryozoan oolite, which outcrops in patches in the low pinelands and sloughs and in the tree island Everglades, Tamiami limestone in Collier and western Monroe counties; and Key Largo limestone (coral rock) in the Florida Keys.

In Dade County these rock surfaces are extremely rough, often forming pinnacle rock. South of Miami, the sinks in the rough limestone are deep (18') and contain much organic matter. The solution holes in the northeast portion of the county are often filled with sand. The rocky soils of Dade County formerly carried fine stands of slash pine and great numbers of tropical hardwood hammocks. Only a few virgin stands of pine and scarcely more than a dozen virgin hammocks today remain in Dade County. The pine stands of the lower Keys growing on Miami oolitic limestone are badly damaged and greatly reduced, but fair samples are still preserved in federal and private sanctuaries, expecially on Big Pine Key.

The coral rock land or Key Largo limestone of the Florida Keys is much harder but was extensively cleared for early pothole farming. The remarkable tropical hardwood forests that were growing there when white man arrived existed because of a deep accumulation of organic debris. These forests have been totally destroyed by repeated fires and bulldozing for developments. A few acres of virgin timber remained on the tip of Key Largo until they were destroyed in 1965. Recent federal legislation approving the Biscayne National Monument should protect the excellent stands of second-growth forests about 35 years of age on Elliott and Rhoades keys. The Key Largo limestone supported several species of tropical hardwoods not found on the mainland; these included red ironwood, lignum vitae, false box, geiger tree, Florida hopbush, and clusia.

The Bryozoan rock outcrops in the low pineland and sloughs carry slash pine and tropical hardwoods. They have not been used for agriculture except by the Seminole Indians, who cleared and planted the tree islands to beans, gourds, corn, and sugarcane during the Indian wars. The second-growth forests coming in on these clearings are even-aged and are sometimes limited to almost pure stands of hackberry, palmetto, potato tree, etc. On most of these sites fragments of Calusa pottery are abundant, indicating an earlier use but probably not much agriculture. Citrus, bananas, and sugarcane may reflect early Spanish introductions. A careful study of the vegetation of these numerous Indian sites and dating of the pottery would undoubtedly reveal much of interest pertaining to Calusa history and the disappearance of this hardy race.

In Collier County, the Tamiami limestone is a much harder rock. It is irregularly broken by sloughs and basins, making it much less attractive to agriculture. Drainage alone would be a tremendous task. These soils carried good stands of pine, cypress, and hardwoods, and should be managed for forest products, game, and recreation. Drought and accompanying fires have been equally destructive, especially those of 1962 and 1965. Some of these rock outcrops have developed typical hammocks resembling those of the Dade rock land, but they are far less numerous, and several of the tropical hardwood species of Dade coastal hammocks and the Florida Keys are lacking. At the present time very little of the Collier County rock land has been developed for agriculture.

Dr. John C. Gifford, a forester who came to Miami about 1900, became much interested in the little known soils and plants of the region. He wrote many articles on pothole farming and forestry during his 50 years in Dade County, of which the following excerpts may be of interest (Gifford, 1946).

A good way to plant these rocky soils is to set little trees in the natural potholes in patches. In the case of lime trees only space enough is needed in between to permit picking. Shelter trees which may be on rock-land between the pot-holes should be left to yield humus and afford shelter against sun and wind, and to furnish homes for birds and other useful creatures. . . . The land that has not been robbed of its trees and fertility is worth several times the bare, rocky areas. . . .

We must not forget that limestone lands demand a covering of vegetation, yielding a constant supply of rich litter. Once in about every ten years in hurricane season the low places are flooded with salt water and banked high with seaweed. This rots and adds to the fertility. . . .

There is an old time system of culture which has its virtues and which might still be practiced with profit with modifications in regions where jungle land is still plentiful. Cut the bush on areas of about five acres in extent. Utilize the logs if the wood is of good quality, or convert it to charcoal which is the favorite fuel of many tropical peoples. Spread the slash evenly over the land. When the ground is moist flash it with fire. Plant therein such crops as corn, pumpkins, melons, tobacco, yucca, pigeon peas or any other desirable crop. In the course of time abandon this patch and let it come back to desirable jungle trees. See to it that it is seeded with the proper kind of trees. The seeds of good kinds can be dibbled in at slight expense. Then select a fresh patch of five acres in some other section and repeat the performance throughout the jungle. In this way forestry and agriculture can be easily and profitably combined. This is a time-honored custom in some sections and if the population is not too dense and the system is worked with care a crop year after year is usually assured. This is separate of course from the home tree garden where food trees of several kinds are usually densely huddled around the house. Closely planted back yard trees are usually the most prolific in all tropical countries. Some trees, like the chocolate, seem to enjoy the social life of the home.

Sandy Soils

Sandy soils are extensive in this three-county area. The northeastern part of Dade, much of Collier County, and western Monroe County inland from the mangrove swamps are predominantly surfaced with thin to deep sandy soils between rock outcrops or marl beds.

In the Big Cypress of Collier and Monroe counties in places where these sands are wet only through the rainy season, slash pine is the predominate tree. Where water stands continuously, as in ponds and sloughs, cypress, water oak, pond apple, and pop ash predominate. Where the sand is higher and infertile, as on ridges and higher coastal dunes, sand pine, scrub oaks, rosemary, and other scrubby hardwoods prevail. Hardwood tree islands are common where Gandy (hammock) peat has built up above the normal water level, but these islands contain mostly swamp species. Much of the pine on the sandy soils south of the Tamiami Trail has been cut or destroyed by fire. In 1962 and 1965 nearly all of the larger blocks of virgin pine south of the Tamiami Trail were seriously damaged. Several pine islands carried beautiful pine stands with some trees as much as 24 inches in diameter. Although slash pine is resistant to fire, hot fires that burn out the debris around the root buttresses are fatal. In this case the cambium on the exposed roots is killed by the heat, defoliation follows, and short new leaves are put out. Such trees often die from bark beetle attacks, which introduce blue stains.

Within Everglades National Park, exposed sandy soils form an element of the beaches of Northwest Cape, Highland Beach, and the Ten Thousand Islands, which extend into Collier County. These sands have been transported from farther north by coastal currents. A considerable deposit of very fine sand lies around the small tributaries of the Broad, Rodgers, and Lostman's rivers. This has been assigned to the Anastasia formation and is covered with a few inches of peat that forms in the saw grass marshes. The tropical hardwoods common to the hammocks on the Flamingo Embankment occur on these sandy beaches with the exception of mahogany and a few others. Their form is short and limby.

In Collier County the Tamiami limestone often meets the inland edge of high tides. Here it is common to see pines and cypress growing side-by-side and red mangrove intermingled in the potholes. Rain water freshens the soil except for the occasional storm tides, and then the saline water drains away or is washed off by the accompanying precipitation. But many such examples of adaptation of plants to the microenvironment occur everywhere in this interesting land.

The agricultural lands of Collier County are primarily on sandy soils; the most extensive area is that around Immokalee. There are many so-called wet prairies scattered over the county, mostly on the lower, poorly drained sands or marls. Sometimes these are broken up for winter crops but are usually soon abandoned.

Marl Soils

Marl soils occur completely around the tip of Florida inside the mangrove belt. Practically all of the area between the Miami oolitic rock ridge and the coastal mangrove belt is surfaced with this type of soil, usually less than 1.5 feet in elevation and 1 to 3 feet to 6 feet deep. It is subject to hurricane tidal overflow, sometimes as far as 10 miles inland. Extensive marl flats also lie landward to the mangroves of the west coast and between the smaller tributaries of the large rivers.

Marl soils during the rainy season become freshwater swamps covered with several species of sedges and grasses. Where the soil is 2 to 3 feet deep and water persists throughout most of the wet years, saw grass is dominant in pure stands, and the marl gives way to beds of peat. On those soils devoid of water during the winter dry season,

Periphyton. *In open sunny glades, especially in the spike rush communities, large patches of floating material rise from the shallow bottom in late summer and form rafts on the water surface. These are periphyton colonies. Periphyton also grows around the stems of plants, forming tube-like structures. Periphyton is composed of numerous one-celled to more complex organisms representing several orders of plants and animals, all held together by several species of algae. A large part of the algae mat is composed of the carbonate mud, calcite, which is precipitated from the water by several of these organisms. These mats are drifted by the wind and lodge among plant stems and on exposed shores, where the organic material breaks down and the carbonates build up the soil. As the organic material disintegrates, the calcite sinks to the bottom, adding an annual layer to the marl stratum from which it originated. Periphyton forms a very important community in the open Everglades. Besides building up the soil, it forms a rich additive that stimulates the growth of grasses and sedges and provides detritus for small aquatic animals. During the recent high waters, the periphyton failed to build up normally, possibly because of the constant movement of the water. On the east side of the Flamingo road, however, the buildup was normal in ponded water during the high water levels of 1968 and 1969.*

sedges, grasses, and spike rushes dominate. Scattered through this belt of marl soil are found large areas where the soil profile shows alternate strata of peat and marl. These are suggestive of long periods, possibly over 100 years, of wet or dry winter climate. From Miami to Homestead most of this marl soil is now protected from hurricane flood tides by the construction of a coastal levee and salt gates, and much of the soil is now under cultivation. Winter potatoes comprise one of the most productive crops. All of the

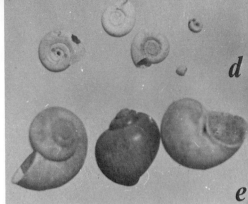

Shells found in freshwater muds. *Some of the shells found in the calcareous deposits of freshwater muds are illustrated here.*
a. *ladder horn shell* (Cerithidea scalariformis)
b. *coffee shell* (Melanopus coffeus)
c. *olive shell* Olivella jaspidia)
d. *sun shell (Helisoma, various species)*
e. *apple shell (Pomacea, various species)*
f. *unidentified*
g. *Carolina marsh clam* (Polymesoda carolineana)
h. *ribbed mussel* (Modiolus americanus)

natural woody vegetation, chiefly swamp trees, has been destroyed. The Australian pine and Brazilian holly quickly seed in on this fallow marl land.

Several types of marl soils, all highly alkaline, have been described. Perrine and Flamingo marls are the most extensive. The latter, chiefly coastal, is largely aragonite deposited under marine conditions, while the freshwater marls are largely calcite. Some of the inland marls have characteristic woody vegetation such as an abundance of cabbage palms. In general, trees are not conspicuous on these soils except for the numerous tree islands; however, they are found in mucky depressions or grow on beds of Gandy peat that has built up beneath them and above the average high water.

The coastal embankments 1.5 to 2.0 feet mean sea level

are formed of marine marl deposited by hurricane tides. This is a fine textured, tough, compacted soil that supports large black mangroves as well as red mangroves where inundated by tidal waters. On the higher (1.5 to 2.0 feet msl) portions of these embankments, organic matter accumulates and eventually—barring fires—tropical hardwoods, including dogwood, mahogany, stoppers, and many other trees, form large hammocks.

The marl soils lying just inside the saline mangrove belt from highway US 1 to Naples in Collier County have not been as extensively cultivated as in Dade County. Much of this land is now within Park boundaries. Outside these boundaries in Collier County the marl flats are quite narrow and broken by rock outcrops. These marl swamps are continuously invaded by red and white mangroves and as frequently are cut back by drought, fire, and frost. The seedlings of neither species can survive if the roots dry out.

The most interesting feature of the extensive marl flats is the numerous tree islands. These are of several types, from the tropical hardwood hammocks where the original limestone has resisted erosion to bay heads on Gandy peat and willow heads and cypress domes or sloughs in wet depressions where water stands on or near the surface throughout the year.

Organic Soils

Formerly much more extensive, organic soils are now found in patches of varying size and are associated with saw grass, juncus (black rush), a few other herbaceous plants, and several species of trees. The most extensive organic soils occur in the tidal lands of the mangrove belt. These have never been fully described and named, but several papers mention a number of types (Spackman, et al., 1966; Scholl, 1967; Craighead, 1964; Llewellyn, 1967).

The organic soils of the mangrove belt are 3 to 15 feet deep and are composed of red mangrove peat or buried mucky peat of former saw grass or juncus marshes. The red mangrove peat may be extremely firm, so much so that the prop roots that form it can no longer penetrate the solid mass. In such places the mangrove trees form a scrubby,

Types of peat soils or sediments. *Peat composes part of the soil in much of the area. It is now usually thin in the freshwater areas where it was once from 3 to 5 feet deep in many places. Several of the different forms of peat may be recognized by the characteristics described and illustrated here.*

a. Red mangrove peat. *Characterized by its reddish color, tiny root hairs, pieces of root bark, and the central vascular bundle of the prop root.*

b. Saw grass peat. *Black, firm to mucky peat, containing scattered bases of saw grass flower stalks.*

c. Joe River peat. *Tough, solid peat 1 to 4 feet deep beneath scrub red mangrove stands. It is composed of tightly compacted materials similar to red mangrove peat, but Joe River peat is found only in the Saline Mangrove Zone.*

d. Hammock peat. *Loose, light brown to darker peat, composed of woody chips and finer organic matter, becoming darker and more compacted with age and depth.*

Muck. *Quite dark to black, often soupy, thickening to a plastic consistency, quite firm and coal-like at lower depths. It is formed from a mixture of finely divided marl and organic matter.*

impenetrable cover 2 to 5 feet tall. In the mangrove flats where the largest trees develop, the peat is a less firm mixture of red mangrove peat and other organic matter to a depth of at least 5 feet. It usually is underlaid by a marl subsoil.

In the freshwater areas are found mucky or peaty soils that are normally covered with water throughout most of the year. These are small to quite large areas scattered where solution holes, sinks, or sloughs etch the bedrock to depths of 1 to 10 feet or more. This black soil is usually mucky, becoming more firm in the dry season. The deeper levels are quite firm and on drying after removal solidify into a hard, coal-like material.

Such soils underlie the saw grass swamps, willow heads, cypress domes, and sloughs, custard apple swamps, and pop ash heads. They are of no agricultural value at present. A high percentage of these organic soils in depressions has been destroyed by fire and oxidation following drainage. These formed one of the chief habitats of the alligator prior to its decimation.

Hammock peat, another form of organic soil, is derived from woody materials and deposited under the tree islands. It occurs under the bay heads of the freshwater areas and the upper river and creek banks and buttonwood strands of the tidal areas. This peat is composed of a surface layer of well aerated, decomposing debris (leaves and branches), and it becomes gradually more compacted and less differentiated in the deeper layers. It is quite friable (easily pulverized) for the first 12 to 18 inches, and contains many small, woody pieces. A large number of trees grow on these sites; the most abundant are buttonwood, poisonwood, dahoon holly, wax myrtle, myrsine, spicewood, mahogany, and randia.

Salinity

The term "soil salinity" is used here in its broad sense, i.e., "total salts," when referring to the response to salinity by plants. Sodium chloride, however, is by far the most important factor in this area in restricting growth and distribution. Many samples of water and soil have been taken over a number of years to determine salinity and its correlation with vegetation.

The salinity of these soils varies tremendously from much above that of seawater to that of fresh water. It varies with each heavy rain as well as seasonally within wide ranges. About one-third of the area is subject to overflow by normal or storm tides, bringing salt waters inland. The plants themselves vary greatly in their tolerance to salt. A few can withstand higher salinities than seawater, and most can tolerate 1,000 parts per million (ppm) for short periods. In general, increasing salinity reduces the availability of water to the plant and slows growth, increases turgidity, causes defoliation, and reduces the size of the leaves or kills the plants outright. These effects as well as the physiology of plant adaptation have been the subjects of some intensive investigation (Bernstein, 1964; Strogonov, 1962; Richards, 1959) and many more restricted studies.

For present purposes, the most important effect of soil salinity is the influence on plant distribution. The surface soils of the intertidal zone are much higher in salts, ranging up to 20,000 ppm or more (Scholl, 1965). During the rainy season, much of the surface soil of the mangrove flats is brackish to fresh, usually below 500 ppm. The fresh water trapped here may last into December or even March in some years. There is also much coastal land and nearby elevations of one-half to several feet where the surface soils are saline only after storm tides. Even in these soils the salts are usually leached from the top 2 to 6 inches a few days later by rainfall (Dalton, 1967, 1968; Llewellyn, 1967).

This wide range of salinity undoubtedly explains the occurrence of many normally freshwater plants in the tidal areas. It also probably accounts for the maximum development of all three species of mangroves in the flats where fresh water is collected and held during the rainy season. Black mangrove, however, does not push very far into the less saline areas.

Very few plants can withstand concentrations of sodium chloride that reach 40,000 to 50,000 ppm. The mangroves, especially the black, and batis (saltwort) and salicornia (glasswort) have this tolerance, while buttonwood is usually destroyed where a concentration of 40,000 ppm is held for a few months. Hurricane Betsy in September 1964, accompanied by very little rainfall, deposited 1 to 2 feet of Florida Bay water on the lower lands behind the coastal levee. Practically all plants died where this water was impounded except for a few red mangroves and batis and salicornia. These survivals were on slight elevations of 0.2 to 0.8 feet, such as humus humps around the bases of trees and rotten logs. It appears also that these plants of high salt tolerance are more vigorous with occasional drenching of fresh water. During the rainy season, these flats are flooded with fresh water that sometimes lasts for as much as six months.

Certain plant adaptations permit adjustments to the varying salinity of these soils. Most of the trees have shallow root systems spread out 2 to 5 inches below the surface. The feeding rootlets are confined to the top 2 to 6 inches of soil and are thus above the higher levels of salinity.

Among the more common species with high tolerance to chlorides that grow around the edges of the salt flats and in the mangrove flats are black, white, and red mangroves, saltwort, glasswort, key grass, salt grass, cord grass, sea blite, crested atriplex, sea purslane, bloodberry, samphire, and careless.

An intermediate group of plants, those growing in the hammocks and on other elevations of the saline zone, are Jamaica dogwood, buttonwood, wild lime, myrsine, solanum, randia, dahoon holly, casuarina, coral bean, red stopper, white stopper, beachberry, and blueweed. Many of these are inland hammock plants, but here the salinity is often around 1,000 ppm and can considerably exceed this for a few days when flooded by storm tides. In this case, the chlorides quickly disappear following the first heavy rain.

In the landward portions of the tidal zone, there are a number of plants in the buttonwood strands and bay heads that tolerate a maximum of around 5,000 ppm; this condition might last for only a short period during the dry season. These are plants that shed a large portion of their leaves. Some of these periodically-deciduous species are dahoon holly, darling plum, red bay, poisonwood, gumbo-limbo, and mahogany. Saw grass and cattails are often killed to the rhizomes and put out new leaves later.

Erosion

This subject has been touched on briefly in the discussion about topography, rock reefs, and tropical hardwood hammocks, but deserves thorough investigation. Limestone outcrops in the pineland and in smaller patches in the higher

Rock gullies. *Rock gullies form a frequent erosion pattern in the Miami oolitic limestone of glades that are 3 feet (msl) or higher. These small gullies were started, like solution holes, some 25,000 years ago, when the sea level was much lower, by the carbonic acid-charged waters percolating through the porous limestone to lower levels. Many plant communities conform to these gullies, as does the saw grass in this picture. Here water remains longer in the dry season, peat accumulates, and saw grass occupies the trenches; the higher adjacent marl or rock land is covered with grasses. As the sea receded thousands of years ago, this entire landscape was no doubt covered with dense stands of mangroves, tropical hardwoods, or saw grass at various stages in relation to the receding waters. This particular glade with the lowered water table of today is now flooded only for short periods during the rainy season. It was dry during the late winter of 1962 when a fire occurred. Water still remains, however, in the deep central solution hole 6 to 10 feet below the surface. Frequently an alligator may remain in such a "well" until the rain replenishes the water in the glades.*

glades are dissected by erosion and broken with numerous solution holes, pinnacle and honeycombed rock, and shallow basins and sloughs of various sizes. This can best be seen after fires remove the organic matter. This topographical pattern of karst was originally formed when the sea level was much lower—25,000 to 50,000 years ago—and still appears to be slowly proceeding. Much of the erosion has taken place underground, forming caves, the roofs of which later collapse to form large solution holes or basins. Such solution holes often follow a slough-like course through the rocky pineland, marking an underground passage, the beginning of a slough. Surface erosion has no doubt been equally important, as shown by the numerous small, rocky mesas projecting above glade level. Often the surface erosion around solution holes takes on a star-like pattern of several fissures draining into a deep, central sinkhole. Small (1929) gave much attention to the erosion of the Miami oolite, which he described and for which he offered explanations of its varied patterns. He attributed this surface karst to the leaching by carbonic and humic acids.

This same irregular erosion pattern is present in the limestone now buried under the soils of the mangrove belt and those of Florida Bay as well, thus antedating the Recent sediments of the mainland.

Egler (1952) noted: "Were both the hammock and peat to be removed from the landscape, the marl surface would be dotted with saucer-like depressions certainly not present as the land arose from the ocean, and not to be ascribed to the currents of the Everglades." This submerged pattern of erosion can easily be demonstrated by taking a line of probes at regular intervals across the overburden of Recent soils. Under this overlay are found solution holes, basins, sloughs, low mesas, and even remains of rock reefs, a perfect duplication of the exposed rock land farther inland. Such features are often defined by characteristic vegetation.

Apparently no serious study of the topography of karst of these South Florida limestones has been undertaken. A number of other tropical limestones, however, have been described and explanations offered for their formation. A recent study by Watson H. Monroe (1966) of deep solution holes or dolines, and ridges or mogotes, seems to apply equally well to local sinkholes, honeycombed and pinnacle rock, and rock reefs. As Monroe states: "In the tropics, beneath a cover of soil the limestone is dissolved rapidly to form deep dolines or cockpits, as the calcium carbonate is carried away in the ground water. In pure limestone not protected by soil, the solutions do not have time to drain from the rock before they are evaporated. As a result,

Pinnacle rock. *Another common erosion feature east of the Big Cypress is pinnacle rock. The erosion shown here was probably formed beneath a cover of peat and vegetation, and is now exposed with the destruction of the peat by repeated fires.*

calcium carbonate is reprecipitated nearly in place to form an indurated capping very resistant to erosion. These effects of solution and induration, largely dependent on soil cover and on purity of the limestone, produce a rugged landscape of a kind well exemplified in northern Puerto Rico."

The exposed portions of local limestones are covered with an indurated capping from several millimeters to several centimeters in thickness. The solution holes, on the other hand, invariably contain a varying quantity of water and soil that concentrate the carbonic acids at the bottom of the hole, where a mass of decomposed, putty-like limestone, easily penetrated with a coring device, is found.

This erosion pattern is also expressed to a considerable extent by the present-day vegetation. In much of the area, particularly in the freshwater swamps where the soil is from 6 to 18 inches deep, the solution holes, basins, and sloughs hold water much longer in the dry season and carry distinctive stands of vegetation, under which an accumulation of peat is preserved. Much of this vegetation is characterized by red mangrove or saw grass growing in scattered clumps. Each small community represents a solution hole, or the larger clumps a basin or former slough where roots can reach moisture in the dry season. As the soil increases in thickness seaward, these isolated clumps tend to coalesce into a continuous stand, until at depths of 4 to 6 feet the soil supports the largest of the mangrove forests. Farther inland, bay heads, cypress heads, and willow heads are likewise growing in these depressions. Even the Florida Bay keys, on the basis of present evidence, overlie shallow basins where the first mangrove clumps would have initiated as the sea rose. Tropical hardwood hammocks occur on rises or mesas of exposed bedrock that were not removed with the general leveling of the limestone.

Observations of numerous burned-out tropical hardwood hammocks near the meeting of the low pineland and glades suggest that these elevated mesas under the tree islands have been protected from erosion by the very shallow layer of humus and give substance to Small's theory that the indurated surface was formed before this recent vegetation appeared. Small (1930a) comments on this and suggests that rain or dew carrying carbonic acid dropping off the leaves has acted on the limestone. It would be interesting to check this experimentally. Small further points out that another type of erosion is due, to some extent, to fires breaking down the calcium carbonate to form readily soluble lime. R. J. Russell and James P. Morgan (1963), in discussing erosion on cliffy coasts, described erosion proceeding high up on these calcareous rocks wherever they are splashed with sea spray that carries carbonic acids. Most of the pH values that have been obtained from samples of the soils of this area are strongly alkaline except for a few determinations around pH 6.5 and 6.6 from subsoil samples.

The so-called tail- or tadpole-shaped tree islands have been commented on by various ecologists. The simplest explanation given is that the "tails" or "grain" represent the direction of drainage and that the "charged" waters moving from the vegetated tree islands erode the tail-like swale in which the vegetation grows. Another explanation seems

Erosion in a limestone sidewalk. *This sidewalk of sawed blocks of Miami oolitic limestone held in place by a concrete mixture was constructed at the home of Mrs. W. J. Krome about 45 years ago. During the ensuing time, atmospheric erosion has lowered the limestone surface about 1 inch below that of the concrete.*

more probable, namely that several tails represented an erosion pattern that occurred early in the development of the solution holes and later one became dominant as a more distinct drainage pattern developed. Many tree islands have two or three spokes of vegetation radiating out from the center as well as the long tails. Generally speaking it seems that the teardrop or tadpole shapes only occur where the present or very recent drainage parallels the grain of the tails.

A remarkable adaptation to this honeycombed limestone is found in many trees, shrubs, and herbs. A bulky subterranean stem develops, forming into the irregularities of the rock. This underground stem resists fire and sends up numerous suckers immediately after the tops are killed. A few of the plants showing this adaptation are mahogany, bustic, blolly, and coontie.

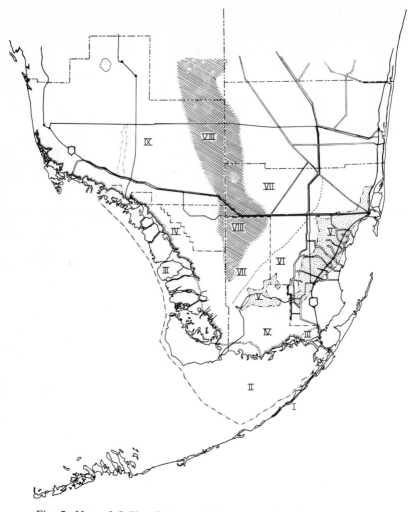

Fig. 7. Map of Collier, Dade, and Monroe counties showing physiographic regions.

    I.   *Florida Keys*
    II.   *Florida Bay*
    III.   *Saline Mangrove Zone*
    IV.   *Freshwater Swamps*
    V.   *Pineland Ridge.*
    VI.   *Low Pineland and Sloughs*
    VII. *Shark River Slough or Tree Island Everglades*
    VIII. *Hammock and Cypress Ridge*
    IX.   *Big Cypress Swamp*

3 ᤒ Physiographic Provinces and Plant Associations

Ecologists, geologists, and agronomists, among others, have descriptively divided the three southern counties of Florida, including the Everglades National Park, into a number of environmental areas called physiographic provinces or ecosystems. The major characteristics of these provinces are their geology, soil, elevation, hydrology, salinity, animals, and vegetation. The latter factor is influenced by all of the other factors and is the basis for the descriptive names chosen for the physiographic provinces described in this text.

Various names have also been used for the some 50 major plant communities, associations, or types found within the physiographic provinces. Each version by a different investigator usually emphasized certain features that that particular writer deemed most important. Some only studied the area for a short period and, since fires, storms, and other physical disturbances frequently cause profound changes in the flora, some descriptions of temporary features have no permanent value. For example, Hurricane Donna in 1960 completely tore away sand and shell beaches in places, leaving a shoreline of peat supporting red, black, and white mangrove trees. A few months later, strong winds from another direction piled up marl, sand, and shell deposits 2 to 5 feet in depth some 75 feet back into the mangrove forest, forming a new beach and killing the mangroves.

In one sense all of these plant associations are temporary. During my years of observation, major changes have been observed in the flora of nearly all of these communities. In an area of such disturbances as hurricanes, frosts, fires, and even the rising sea, a climax community lasts for but a relatively short time.

The hurricane of 1935 wiped out one of the oldest (probably 250 years of age) and best developed black mangrove forests in the entire area. This was replaced by a dense stand of red mangrove that later was completely destroyed in 1960 by Hurricane Donna. Ten years later, the area now is almost completely covered by grasses, sedges, cattails, batis, and careless; this vegetation now competes with mangrove reproduction.

Many factors influencing such division have been considered, and my descriptive names have been chosen to express the dominant characteristics of each. Some of these terms are based on names suggested by earlier workers, including Harshberger (1914), Harper (1927), Small (1930-1950), Davis (1940-1943), Jones (1948), Loveless (1959), Spackman et al. (1966), and Scholl and Stuiver (1967).

Each of the nine physiographic provinces will be briefly described and characterized in terms of its overall geology, soil, hydrology, and vegetation, and then the principal plant communities existing within the province will be given detailed attention. Pertinent, additional physiographic details of these sub-regions are presented as well as a listing of characteristic plant species found in each. Some plant communities appear in more than one physiographic province and when this is the case, the community is sometimes described only once, on its first appearance, and cross references to it used later.

PROVINCE I – FLORIDA KEYS

The long string of islands curving southwest for over 100 miles from Key Biscayne to the Dry Tortugas composes this province. The upper keys extend to Key Vaca, the lower keys from Bahia Honda Key through Key West. The Marquesas and the Dry Tortugas, characterized by deep deposits of sand, shell, and muck, are not considered in this treatment.

Geology

The upper keys are composed largely of coral Key Largo limestone of Pleistocene age, formed about 27,000 years ago. This coral outcrops from mean sea level to some 8 to 10 feet above. It presents a roughly eroded surface pitted with numerous solution holes. In places it is covered with quartz sand. The lower keys are composed of Miami oolitic limestone of the lower Sangamon period, about 100,000 years of age.

Soil and Hydrology

The upper keys have an alkaline soil, of Recent age (5,000 years or less), composed of disintegrated coral rock mixed with organic materials, shell, and some quartz sand in the rock cavities. Red mangrove peat 2 to 6 feet deep lies under the coastal mangrove swamps. Formerly, soil of hammock peat 12 to 18 inches thick covered this limestone and supported rich tropical forests. The area is watered by rainfall, about 25 to 50 inches annually, and parts are occasionally covered by hurricane tides.

The soil of the lower keys consists of disintegrated Miami oolitic limestone mixed with shell, organic matter, and considerable sand. Also watered by rainfall of 25 to 35 inches a year, precipitation on the lower keys decreases toward Key West.

Vegetation

On the upper keys, the uplands carry tropical hardwoods, especially gumbo-limbo, mastic, poisonwood, lysiloma, velvetleaf, crabwood, and lignum vitae. The small bays and coves bear algae and sea grasses, and inland, water-holding depressions support freshwater swamp plants.

On the lower keys are found stands of Dade County (slash) pine, tropical hardwoods, and several trees not found on the upper keys, such as gyminda, savia, pisonia, and clusia. There are numerous thatch and silver palms as well.

Plant Associations

In the upper keys, two plant associations, Tropical Hardwood Hammocks and Mangrove Swamps, occupy most of the area. In the lower keys the more important plant associations are Tropical Hardwood Hammocks, Mangrove Swamps, Lower Keys Pineland, and Tidal Flats. Small Saw Grass Marshes (see p. 140) are frequent in the pineland depressions.

Tropical Hardwood Hammocks

High (1.5 to 10 feet msl), well-drained coral rock pitted with numerous sinks formerly covered with 6 to 18 inches of hammock peat and litter support these hammocks. The principal tree species in the upper keys are Jamaica dogwood, gumbo-limbo, lysiloma, milkbark, Guiana plum, crabwood, torchwood, wild cinnamon, blolly, saffron plum, mastic, Florida boxwood, geiger tree, mahogany, sea grape, dove plum, black and white ironwood, bay cedar, and poisonwood. Those of the lower keys are slash pine, savia, gyminda, dodonaea, joewood, brysonima, custard apple, silver palm, two species of thatch palm, cabbage palm, and saw palmetto.

Mahogany. *Illustrated is a tropical hardwood hammock on north Key Largo. Large mahogany crowns top the other trees. Many are infested by a mistletoe that appears to be gradually killing them. Fires, clearing of land, and selective logging for ship knees and other materials account for the almost complete destruction of these fine tropical forests that once contained over 100 species of trees.*

Mangrove stand on Matecumbe Key. *Once a well-developed forest with some trees 2 feet in diameter and over 150 years old, this mangrove stand was finally destroyed by Hurricane Donna in 1960. It had previously escaped many hurricanes, including the great Labor Day hurricane of September 1935.*

Mangrove Swamps

These swamps are similar on both the upper and lower keys, and are low (0.0 to 0.5 feet msl) coastal areas of red mangrove peat 2 to 6 feet deep that have been built up with the rising sea. The principal trees are red, black, and white mangrove and mangrove mallow, a shrub. Buttonwood occurs where the peats have built up slightly above (10") mean sea level.

Lower Keys Pineland

Well-drained oolitic limestone pitted with solution holes and sinks bearing marl or peat characterize this plant association. Distinctive vegetation includes Dade County pine, silver palm, and two species of thatch palms, with tropical hardwoods growing on the accumulations of peat.

Tidal Flats

Low marl flats covered by high tides are frequent. They may be of considerable size and form bay-like areas in the pineland. Key grass is a constant dominant on these flats.

PROVINCE II – FLORIDA BAY

This large area, roughly 35 by 50 miles, is partly enclosed by the Florida Keys and the mainland. It is a shallow depression from 3 to 15 feet deep of highly saline water, up to 50 parts per thousand. It is characterized by large mud flats about mean sea level in elevation, low islands called keys, and scattered deeper channels and basins of shallow water varying in depth from 3 to 9 feet.

Geology

The bedrock of Florida Bay is Miami oolitic limestone from the late Pleistocene or Key Largo limestone. This is overlaid by mud banks and keys of Recent origin.

Soil and Hydrology

The mud flats are composed of marl and shell 3 to 8 feet deep. They are exposed at low tide, providing a rich feeding ground for many birds. The keys, built up in depressions of the bedrock of marl and mangrove peat, are deeper by 1 to 3 feet than the bedrock of the flats.

The area is watered by high tides and rainfall. The low interiors of the Florida Bay keys may have ponds of fresh or brackish water during the rainy season.

Vegetation

Mud banks support several marine flowering plants, especially turtle grass and also marine algae. On the keys, mangrove swamps and mangrove perimeters support numerous tropical hardwoods on the more elevated areas, plus various shrubs, sedges, and grasses.

Plant Associations

There are three principal plant associations in this province: Mud Flats, Florida Bay Keys, and Submarine Meadows.

Mud Flats

Mud Flats, or Turtle Grass Beds, are from 4 to 8 feet deep to bedrock and often one-third of the volume is

Calusa Key. *This photograph was taken two years after Hurricane Donna to show the destruction of the woody vegetation, chiefly mangrove, that was established in the central pond. Many of the perimeter trees escaped destruction. The background and exposed land surrounding this key show mud flats, or banks, at low tide. The mud flats of Florida Bay make up nearly one-half of the area. They are from 5 to 8 feet deep and are gradually building up with calcareous deposits. At low tide these flats are out of the water and at high tide are submerged. They are formed of carbonate muds, chiefly aragonite and high magnesium calcites precipitated by living algae. Several species of flowering plants, especially turtle grass, are abundant. The mud binds together large amounts of animal skeletons, shells, foraminifera, and calcareous plant remains. These mud flats support an enormous variety and number of plant and animal species. They are an important resource that is gradually being destroyed by high powered speed boats, whose propellers cut out swaths in the grass beds, which then become further enlarged by tidal action.*

marine shell, foraminifera, and calcareous plant remains suspended in a very finely divided marl-like mud. The mud flats of Florida Bay, often several miles across, are carpeted and held in place by marine flowering plants and algae. Many square miles of these mud flats are exposed at low tide.

The principal flowering plants of this community are turtle grass, horned pondweed, sea grass, and manatee grass. Many algae are present, including species of halimeda, caulerpa, batophora, and sargassum (Taylor, 1954; Thorne, 1954; Tabb and Manning, 1961).

Clive Key. *Two years after Hurricane Donna many mangroves survived and new seedlings have become established on the battered perimeter of this key. The high grassy prairie to the left and the gradually filling pond, now spotted with young mangrove trees, in the right center is a characteristic stage in the development of these offshore keys. These islands, originally bay heads in a freshwater swamp, have been building up with the rising sea for the past 5,000 years. They are protected from hurricane tides by the perimeter mass of stiff red mangrove peat, and the center is built up with finely particulate hurricane mud and carbonate muds precipitated by the algae mats in the ponded center.*

Florida Bay Keys

These islands are of two kinds. One type, chiefly in the northeastern part of Florida Bay, has a profile of surface peat 3 to 5 feet thick above 1 to 2 feet of marl and is usually covered with mangrove forests. The other type, more numerous, has a perimeter of mangrove enclosing a depressed central area composed of stiff, dense, hurricane mud, chiefly aragonite, of very fine particle size and containing practically no shell. The fringe of mangroves is underlaid with tough red mangrove peat. This rim rises inland to form an embankment 1 to 2 feet above normal high tides. Here tropical hardwoods are found.

The genesis of the atoll-like Florida Bay keys was prior to the sea rise of some 5,000 years ago. The keys have persisted because of the stormproof wall of red mangrove peat that has gradually built up with the rising sea (see p. 35). The interior ponds that fill with hurricane mud never quite catch up to the height of the perimeter. Any vegetation is periodically killed by hurricane mud deposits. During the rainy season the water in these ponds is low in salt content and supports a mat-like bed of periphyton (Craighead, 1969).

On the well-drained soil of these keys several species of grasses, shrubs, and tropical hardwoods are found. On a number of keys the hammock areas are rather extensive and impressive. The floral composition of these is quite similar to that of the mainland. Some species, such as maytenus and tall sandspur, are distinctive of the central areas, and key grass characterizes the tidal flats. The moon vine often grows luxuriantly, covering some of the hammock growth.

Vines becoming dominant on Dildo Key. *Vines are a conspicuous feature of and play an important role in nearly all plant communities of the area. In the saline mangrove swamps and on the keys in Florida Bay, several vines immediately became dominant after Hurricane Donna defoliated the forest communities, permitting sunlight to reach the soil. The stored seeds germinated, and the vines spread over the broken tropical hardwood trees. In this case on Dildo Key, the moon vine* (Calonyction tuba) *completely covers a stand of bumelia previously used as a rookery by cormorants. These birds continued nesting, as was evident by their alarmed attitudes on the approach of the photographer.*

Submarine Meadows

Throughout Florida Bay are numerous areas deeper (3 to 6 feet) than the surrounding mud; these may be several acres in extent and are called "holes" or, when larger in area, "lakes" by the local fishermen. The floor is limestone in the northeastern portions of the bay and mud from 1 to several feet thick in the western portions. These areas are often covered with seaweeds and were termed "Submarine Meadows" by Thorne (1954). The vegetation is composed of several species of flowering plants and algae that can endure the deeper water and the more murky light conditions existing there.

PROVINCE III – SALINE MANGROVE ZONE

This crescent-shaped province extends inland approximately 15 miles along the Shark River and narrows to the east and west to a few hundred yards in width in the Miami area and in northwestern Collier County. At both ends this crescent narrows to within a few yards at the points where it meets the pine-covered rock land. North of Cape Sable this zone is characterized by deep estuaries that divide into numerous freshwater creeks and penetrate the freshwater zone. This province was termed "Paralic Swamps" by Scholl and Stuiver (1967).

South of Cape Sable the shoreline is broken only by a few creeks that bisect the well-defined coastal (Flamingo) embankment that rises 1 to 2 feet above mean sea level. Along the west coast north of the Lostman's River the shore is broken into numerous keys collectively called the Ten Thousand Islands. Here the surface deposit of red mangrove peat is 2 to 4 feet thick and lies on a deep (10 to 15 feet) deposit of quartz sand and shell. This coast is slowly eroding. Each severe hurricane cuts away some sand from under this peat and topples the mangroves into the Gulf. Degradation from the rising sea is proceeding more rapidly here than in the tough marl shores of Florida Bay, where, in addition, wave action is less intense.

Along the inner edge of the Saline Mangrove Zone lies a

string of lakes and bays from US 1 to Naples on the west coast. On the landward shore of these waters is a low levee called the "Buttonwood Embankment" (Craighead, 1964) separating the saline waters from the inland freshwater swamps. At places this embankment has been destroyed by fires and permits the intrusion of high tides into former freshwater areas. This has happened three times since 1962. This area is a fertile nursery ground for wildlife and of great economic value because of the fisheries that it supports.

Geology

The bedrock, which is 2 to 15 feet deep, is composed of Bryozoan (Hoffmeister, et al., 1967) or Miami limestone east of the Shark River, and of Tamiami limestone on the west coast. The overburden is composed of marl, shell, sand, and peat, and is of Recent origin. It is of organic genesis except for the quartz sand, which is transported from farther north by longshore drift.

Soil and Hydrology

The soils of the eastern portion of the Saline Mangrove Zone north of Florida Bay are deep, tough, aragonitic marls deposited by hurricanes and forming a coastal ridge, the Flamingo Embankment, 1 to 2 feet above mean sea level. This is often only 100 yards in width, but near Flamingo these higher deposits extend inland for a mile or more (see USC&GS Map 598SC). Behind this coastal levee, extensive deposits of mangrove peat and marl occur under the mangrove forests. On the west coast, over much of this zone deep sand takes the place of the marl beds.

In general the soils—the term is used here for the entire overburden on the bedrock—in this zone are deep, 6 to 15 feet near the coast, tapering inland to the Buttonwood Embankment where they may be 4 to 6 feet in thickness. They are composed of red mangrove peat under the mangroves along the river banks. Between the rivers, muck or saw grass peat lies under the juncus swamps. These are stratified with marine deposits of marl or sand on the west coast. Much marine shell, probably associated with old estuaries, is found in certain places.

The area is watered by saline tides, but the interiors of

the islands and marshes usually hold fresh to brackish (15 % salts) water during the rainy season. On these mangrove flats, alternately saline and fresh, the best developed mangrove stands are found. They also provide the abundant shrimp and food fishes that attract many species of birds to this winter feeding ground.

Vegetation

The dominant plants are the three mangroves—red, white, and black—which reach their greatest size on the tidal flats, and the usual halophytes. Many of the tropical hardwoods grow on the higher, well-drained ground, namely the coastal embankment and shell mounds. Black mangrove is widely distributed but does not extend inland entirely across the tidal zone where this belt is wide. White mangrove occurs on all lowlands and invades the freshwater area 1 to 3 miles, while red mangrove pushes landward 10 to 15 miles into the cypress and to the edge of the pine association.

The banks of the estuaries are forested with mangroves for a few miles upstream from the coast. Farther inland, as the water becomes less brackish, buttonwood and swamp hardwoods dominate the creek banks, Between these wooded banks lie extensive swamps filled with a mucky to peaty soil 6 to 9 feet deep. Overhanging mats of juncus and other sedges and grasses are gradually filling the numerous ponds of these swamps. As the surface rises, buttonwood strands and islands form.

The ability of red mangrove to invade far into the freshwater areas has caused much confusion in the interpretation of these zones and has resulted in expensive engineering mistakes. The common interpretation has been to call any area supporting red mangroves a marine environment. For this reason it seems logical to separate the saline and freshwater swamps even though red mangrove populates thousands of acres of the latter.

Plant Associations

Thirteen principal plant associations of Province III will be described; they are: Beaches and Mangrove Shores; Batis Marshes; Buttonwood or Madeira Hammocks; Saline Buttonwood Islands and Strands; Shell Mounds; Marl or Coastal Prairies; Cape Sable Hammocks; Cape Sable Prairies; Ponds; Mangrove Flats; Scrub Mangrove; Juncus Marshes; and River Banks.

Beaches and Mangrove Shores

In the shallow and relatively calm waters of the bays, bights, and minor indentations surrounding the tip of Florida, the shoreline is more frequently occupied by arborescent plants than by beaches. Were it not for the occasional hurricane, practically the entire shoreline would be forested. Many miles of beaches that formerly had a fringe of mangroves are now deforested, pushed back 50 to 100 feet by the 1935 and 1960 hurricanes. Scattered large, dead, black mangrove trees remain to mark the former shoreline, which is gradually receding with the rising sea. (See pp. 35, 38, and 42.) The new shores are often piled with a dense mass of seaweeds 1 to 2 feet thick. Much of this mass is continually seething with the tide and offers poor anchorage to mangrove seedlings. Some seedlings, however, are carried over the barrier by high equinoctial tides and become established.

Probably two-thirds of the shoreline from Miami to

Turtle grass. *This beach of tough marl is covered with 12 inches of turtle grass that rises and seethes with each high tide. Mangrove seedlings cannot become established in such a situation. The red, white, and black mangroves were established when this beach was much wider. Patches of salt joint grass* (Paspalum vaginatum) *are also shown.*

Island near Coon Key. *This is one of the Ten Thousand Islands near Coon Key in Collier County. Hurricane Donna destroyed the mangroves and buttonwood on this outer island, and removed about 2 feet of red mangrove peat. Remains of prop roots can be seen projecting above the sand. In the Ten Thousand Islands, the substrate below the peat is fine quartz sand instead of marl, as in Florida Bay. Soil profiles show patches of red mangrove peat, indicating this process has been repeated several times in the past.*

Black mangrove shoreline. *These mangroves, chiefly black, near Shark River Point are characteristic of a receding shoreline. Some storms deposit sand and marl around the bases of the shoreline trees, causing their death.*

Everglades City is concealed by red or black mangroves in about equal proportions. Red mangrove, often called the pioneer species, is no doubt somewhat better adapted to make the initial colonization. It is more susceptible, however, to destruction by hurricanes, and this results in some areas in an increased proportion of black mangroves. At some places along the coast, such as at the mouth of the Shark, Big Sable, and Broad rivers, the shoreline is receding, and black mangroves of large size stand in water or at the water's edge.

Soil. The soils of the beaches or shorelines are composed of limestone in the Miami area and the upper and lower Keys, with occasional deposits of quartz sand. Nearly all of the Florida Bay keys have marl shorelines except those shores facing open, deeper water, where finely broken shell forms calcareous beaches superimposed on marl.

The marl shoreline continues to Cape Sable, becoming more shelly northward and carrying a considerable proportion of quartz sand on northwest Cape Sable. From there to Naples, quartz sand dominates, with varying amounts of shell.

These shorelines are in a continuous process of change, chiefly the result of hurricane tides and the rising sea. Mangrove peat lies buried under 3 feet of shell and sand and 3 to 4 feet of water 1 mile off the Shark and Broad rivers (Spackman, et al., 1966), and the present shoreline to the rear is a mangrove forest often with 1.5 to 5.0 feet of shell piled up among the trees from hurricanes Donna in 1960 and Betsy in 1965. Behind the immediate strand subject to normal tides, all beaches quickly build up inland for several hundred feet to elevations of from 2 to 5 feet (msl), with tidal and storm deposits of marl, shell, or sand, depending on the location.

The most extensive beaches in Everglades National Park are those connecting the three capes (East, Middle, and Northwest) and Highland Beach; the former extends for about 10 miles along Cape Sable, the latter for 6 miles between Lostman's and Broad rivers. They are primarily marl with much shell and some quartz sand. Profiles show that at times in the past, probably within the past 1,000 to

2,000 years, quartz composed a much larger proportion than at present.

Behind the Cape Sable beaches lies a coastal prairie, up to 1,800 feet wide, composed of a succession of shallow troughs and low dunes (Craighead and Gilbert, 1962). To the rear on the highest elevations (4 to 5 feet msl) is a continuous ridge of hammock plants. At places these beaches are receding toward the mangrove swamps to the rear, leaving mangrove stumps offshore. In one section the hammock strip now fronts the ocean. Highland Beach is also composed of shell and sand over a marl base. This beach was raised to a height of 6 feet at places by Hurricane Donna. Behind this beach is a mangrove flat some half mile wide and another, and much higher, shell dune broken at places by creeks but practically paralleling the present shoreline. This structure requires more study and comparison with other inland shell mounds and their underlying oyster bars. Highland Beach is now a solid stand of casuarina, whose seeds were brought in by Hurricane Donna.

Vegetation. The vegetation of these shorelines varies considerably with the soil and the salt tolerance of the plants. Some of the more characteristic trees and shrubs of the beaches and coastal ridges are randia, buttonwood, Jamaica dogwood, casuarina, seven-year apple, sea grape, joewood, bay cedar, beachberry, yucca, beach elder, sea lavender, Christmasberry, necklace pod, saltwort, sea daisy, mangrove, coconut, catsclaw, coral bean, white and Spanish stoppers, myrsine, and saffron plum. Among the herbaceous plants the following are common: sea oats, broom sedges, salt grass, sandspurs, key grass, panic grass, beach grass, big cord grass, dropseed (mat grass), sea blite, sesuvium, crested atriplex, samphire, railroad vine, species of moonflowers, poor-man's patch, dildoe, and opuntia.

Batis Marshes

At many places where the coastal embankments slope landward into the mangrove flats, the lowering marl soils are covered with almost pure beds of batis mixed with other fleshy halophytes and often spotted with scrubby red, white, and black mangroves. The soil may be covered seasonally with either fresh or salt water except in the late

Batis marsh. *This photograph, taken on the Flamingo Prairie just north of the Buttonwood Bridge, illustrates the density of a batis ground cover. Mangrove seedlings as well as other woody plants rarely become established in such a community until it is destroyed by a hurricane.*

winter, when the surface is often dry. Harper (1927) described this association under the name "Salt Flats," and they have also been called "Salt Marshes."

This association grades into the mangrove flats and, in fact, is a temporary type, finally replaced by mangroves, chiefly black mangrove. Following Hurricane Donna in 1960, the seed of batis immediately germinated and formed an almost continuous ground cover throughout the entire saline zone on low tidal lands where the mangrove stands had been killed and sunlight reached the new soil left by the storm tide. Batis is a light-demanding plant that was relatively scarce before Hurricane Donna in all well stocked mangrove forest areas. The seeds float and were widely distributed in the fresh mud deposits. By the end of the second summer following this storm, practically the entire area of destruction could be distinguished from the air by the yellowish-green ground cover of this scrubby plant.

The stems of batis loop over and intertwine to reach a

height of from 2 to 3 feet, making a tangle that is very difficult to penetrate. This mat is an effective hindrance to the growth of mangrove seedlings. On hurricane study plots, the growth of such seedlings was suppressed and many of them died before the end of the second year.

Soil. This association is confined to low (plus or minus 0.3 to 0.5 feet msl), highly saline, marl soils often of considerable depth (7 to 10 feet) near the coastal embankment. When it grades into the mangrove flats, deep strata of red mangrove muck and peat occur, as described in the discussion of mangrove flats (p. 110).

Vegetation. The fleshy-leaved halophytes, glasswort, sea blite, sea purslane, careless, and samphire are associated with batis, but in time are slowly retarded or crowded out by the batis. On the higher edges of the batis flats that blend into the coastal prairies, sea daisy and cord grass often replace batis.

Buttonwood or Madeira Hammocks

It is apparent that prior to white man's activities, the coastal embankments along Florida Bay were completely occupied by buttonwood and other tropical hardwoods. The best evidence for this is the abundance of tree snail shells, Liguus and Oxostylus, in the surface soil of the prairies as well as in the forested portions.

Prairies of shrubby growth and immature buttonwood now occur on much of the coastal levee around the tip of Florida. Buttonwood is the first tree to invade the soil cleared for charcoal hearths or agriculture. Later these stands become infiltrated with a number of tropical hardwoods. Among the first are Spanish stopper, saffron plum, and randia. Once mahogany was abundant, as evidenced by the term "Madeira Hammocks" and numerous madeira stumps still remaining.

Before the 1935 hurricane this coastal levee, extending from northwest Cape Sable to Crocodile Point, supported considerable mahogany, Jamaica dogwood, and other hardwoods. Cabbage palm was abundant and of large size. The mahogany was tall, with straight trunks and clear boles for 20 to 40 feet. Residents who lived in the area prior to 1935 described the wood as straight-grained and of superior quality for ship building. This feature no doubt resulted in the "high grading" and removal of the better trees over a period of perhaps 200 years or more.

Soil. The soil supporting these coastal hammocks is a gray to bluish marl 6 to 12 feet deep. It is of a fine, tough, uniform consistency with few marine shells, but it may have lenses of red mangrove peat at various levels. The surface half-foot becomes quite friable from the breakdown of organic matter, and forms a very productive soil that formerly sustained trees up to 2 and 3 feet in diameter. Fires and hurricanes have removed this rich topsoil to practically bare marl. Remnants left on some of the mounds indicate a former surface of loam of 10 inches or more.

Vegetation. Floristically, this association, like the shell mounds and the Cape Sable hammocks, is richest in species of all of the Saline Mangrove Zone communities. The trees include mahogany, Jamaica dogwood, gumbo-limbo, poison-wood, mastic, royal palm, cabbage palm, satinleaf, coral bean, dove plum, blolly, black ironwood, two kinds of figs, wild lime, randia, acacia, saffron plum, myrsine, wild cinnamon, manchineel, soapberry, foresteria, Spanish stopper, white stopper, nakedwood, caper, hog plum, paurotis palm, inkwood, and catsclaw. In addition, a number of shrubs, vines, and herbaceous plants, such as nicker bean, hippocratea, sarcostemma, rubber vine, and moonflowers are abundant.

Fauna. Early records indicate an abundant wildlife, especially deer, which were still present from 1950 through 1955 but are practically absent today. Bears and mountain lions were once present. Bobcats are still numerous, as well as raccoons and swamp rabbits. Rattlesnakes were common in the early fifties but are rarely seen now.

Saline Buttonwood Islands and Strands

The numerous buttonwood tree islands scattered through the swampy areas of Province III are here described as a plant association distinct from the buttonwood stands on the deep coastal marl levees and the bay heads of the freshwater zone. These islands are numerous north of Whitewater Bay.

Soil. The soil is composed of hammock peat built up to

elevations of 1.5 to 3.0 feet above mean tide; it is submerged by storm tides. Small, abrupt elevations from 1 to 2 feet may well be old alligator nest remains from a freshwater past. This peat may be 2 to 3 feet deep on top of marl deposits, or, as in the case of numerous islands north of Whitewater Bay, the peaty soils often extend to bedrock, indicating a history of 4,000 years.

Vegetation. Buttonwood forms nearly pure stands on the islands and strands (ribbon-like formations) that have built up a peaty elevation of a foot or more, as in the vicinity of Whitewater Bay. Where these stands are more open they carry the usual assortment of halophytes. Farther inland, the somewhat salt-tolerant plants randia, bumelia, Spanish stopper, Christmasberry, and leather fern appear among the buttonwoods, and nearer the buttonwood levee, where only the occasional hurricane tide inundates them, a wide assortment of freshwater plants comes in, including pepper vine, possum grape, moonflowers, hippocratea, Virginia creeper, poison ivy, rubber vine, grapes, dove plum, coco plum, poisonwood, wax myrtle, red bay, mahogany, wild lime, cattails, and many air plants, bromeliads, and orchids.

Shell Mounds

The numerous shell mounds, or Indian mounds, of the Saline Mangrove Zone are here described as a distinct plant

Shell mounds. *Shell mounds are found along or near the coast around the tip of Florida. Most of these were occupied by pre-Columbian Indians. White men later farmed many of them. Some retain a relatively rich flora. This photo was taken on Mound Key in Collier County*

Gopher Key. *Probably the largest of over 100 mounds in the Everglades National Park, Gopher Key is shown here immediately after Hurricane Donna had killed most of the surrounding vegetation.*

community. They form the highest elevations in the area—5 to 25 feet—and Chokoloskee Island, which has over 100 acres of shell, attains an elevation of about 40 feet at one site.

The oldest and largest mounds are inland 1 to 2 miles along the chain of lakes and bays. When first formed, possibly before the earliest occupation by Indians, they were no doubt on or close to the shore. Those examined by the writer are landward to buried oyster bars now 2 to 3 feet below the surface (msl), from which the initial elevations were built by storm tides.

Nearly all the mounds show evidence of occupation by aborigines, and considerable shell accretion was undoubtedly from these people. Some mounds show stratification of clean shell from storm tides and organic layers of so-called "Indian soil" (Craighead, 1964). Hurricane Donna in 1960 piled as much as 16 inches of shell on top of the coastal

Lostman's River oyster bar. *Oyster bars or beds are a characteristic feature of the mouths of most estuaries. They form extensive flats 18 to 24 inches thick on top of the deltic mud, which is sometimes 15 feet deep. The bars partially block most of the entrances to the deeper inland channels of the mangrove rivers, requiring careful attention in navigation. They often form long, torturous reefs in inland bays, where they also obstruct small craft navigation. These oyster beds were the source of much of the shell piled up on Indian mounds by hurricanes. In probing to examine inland soil structures, these beds are frequently discovered buried 1 to 3 feet, especially just seaward to shell mounds.*

Oyster shell islands. *Mangrove islands (good examples are near Rookery Bay, Collier County) often develop on mud flats, and soon the prop roots serve as attachments for coon oysters. One to 3 feet of dead shell may build up beneath the roots, forming firm islands on top of a marl or sand substrate. At some places, erosion from the wash of boats at low tide tears out the mud binder among the shells and loosens the prop roots. Many mangrove islands are now disappearing along the much traveled canals and the Intracoastal Waterway, leaving shell islands.*

mounds around the mouth of Lostman's River. This material came from the extensive oyster bars formed on top of the deep mud banks just offshore from the river's mouth.

Soil. Many of these mounds were occupied by white man and were farmed from 1870 until the rich humus soil was destroyed and the growing of crops no longer profitable (Simpson, 1920, 1923). Some of those mounds first "farmed out" by white man have rebuilt an organic soil, and a very few have escaped this ruinous cultivation. The deep, shelly mixture of dark brown organic matter and broken shell provides one of the most fertile sites in the mangrove country. It is well drained and well aerated, but because of the high shell content it is exceedingly difficult to sample with any tool.

Vegetation. All of the mounds are now covered with vegetation, chiefly tropical hardwood trees. Among the more common are gumbo-limbo, dove plum, sea grape, mastic, figs, poisonwood, myrsine, bustic, paradise tree, nakedwood, Spanish and white stoppers, saffron plum, royal palm, cabbage palm, black ironwood, canella, ardisia, foresteria, inkwood, two species of capers, and manchineel.

There is a greater number of plant species present on these mounds than in any other plant association of this zone. Undoubtedly the Indians used many of the plants for food or medical purposes. Several of the legumes with a high derris content—Jamaica dogwood, two species of dalbergia, and soapberry—were used as fish poisons and are almost always present on these sites.

Marl or Coastal Prairies

Often on the coastal embankments a prairie-like vegetation of grasses and shrubs will be found. This association occurs in patches on well-drained (in the sense that the water runs off quickly), deep, marl soil built up 1.5 to 2.0 feet above mean sea level. It is found from Crocodile Point around the mainland, and on intermittently north behind the Ten Thousand Islands to Naples. Some of these prairies are extensive and have acquired local names, such as the Flamingo and Raulerson prairies. Other patches are small and scattered among the buttonwoods. There is much

Coastal prairie. *Uninfluenced by man or fire, this prairie would be occupied by buttonwood and tropical hardwood forests. Prior to 1900 much of it carried excellent stands of mahogany. Probably as early as 1800, charcoal operations in the buttonwood stands, culling for the finest mahogany, and later agricultural activities cleared much of the forest lands around Flamingo. Shrubby and herbaceous species then occupied the ground, and repeated fires prevented reestablishment of the hardwoods. The dense ground cover is now composed of sea daisy, opuntia, yucca, batis, thoroughworts, cord grass, and several other grasses and sedges. The darker patch to the middle left marks the site of an old charcoal hearth. These can often be recognized by the contrasting vegetation that grows on charcoal beds. The high, chopped-off stumps are also an indication of early clearing for charcoaling.*

evidence to show that these prairies were formerly covered with hammock growth, and that this low, herbaceous, and shrubby growth resulted from clearing and fires. Numerous tree snail shells can be turned up in the surface soil with slight digging.

Extensive areas of buttonwood hammocks were cleared for charcoal production. Many charcoal hearths where the wood was burned are still visible. All are older than forty years, and some probably go back 200 years. A few of these charcoal hearths have been pierced when taking cores of the soil. The deepest one found to date was covered by 11 inches of marl deposited by hurricanes. During the charcoaling and agricultural days prior to the establishment of the

Park in 1947, fires during the dry season were commonly associated with all of these activities as the simplest means of clearing the land.

Vegetation. Two species of plants form most of the cover on these praries, *Spartina spartinae* or tall cord grass, locally called switch grass, and *Borrichia frutescens,* seaside daisy or blueweed. These finally assume dominance and form pure stands over most of the prairie area.

In the ten years since Hurricane Donna, many of these prairies have been extensively invaded by other plants, chiefly buttonwood. The layer of marl mud furnished a good seedbed among the shattered plants and at the same time deposited floatable seeds in the area. With the protection from fires that is now part of Park policy, most of these shrubby prairies will be reforested in the near future.

Cape Sable Hammocks

To the rear of the three capes that comprise Cape Sable and behind the shelly prairie is an almost continuous strip

Charcoal hearth. *This cone of piled buttonwood trunks and branches shows the last of the charcoal operations on the Flamingo Prairie. It was covered with marl and all ready to fire when the Labor Day hurricane came along in 1935. The top tier of sticks and mud was removed. Then Hurricane Donna in 1960 took away more, leaving the kiln as seen here.*

Buttonwood stand. *This 10 year old stand of buttonwood is 22 feet tall and many trees are 2 to 3˘ inches in diameter at the base. Hurricane Donna destroyed much of the shrubby ground cover and distributed buttonwood seed in the 5 inch layer of hurricane mud the storm deposited. The buttonwood seedlings developed rapidly, and many such patches sprang up throughout the coastal prairies.*

of tropical hardwood hammock about 10 miles long. It is broken by the erosion of the encroaching sea at two points. Its width ranges from a few feet to about 300 feet behind Northwest Cape and East Cape.

Soil. The organic debris has been carried to and deposited along this strand of trees by many hurricanes. Thus, gradually, a rich, well-drained, loamy soil has been built up. Considerable marl and some little sand are mixed in the decomposing vegetable matter, forming a grayish to black, nutritious soil not seen elsewhere in the Park. This is underlaid by a dense hurricane marl and sand, reaching to bedrock 9 to 10 feet below. Strata of fine quartz sand must have been much more evident 1,000 to 2,000 years ago than on the present beaches.

Vegetation. Plant growth is luxuriant, resembling that of

the shell mounds. Papayas reached a height of 25 feet with basal diameters to 7 inches the first season after Hurricane Donna. Cacti, yucca, and agave are abundant, at times forming inpenetrable thickets. Harper (1927, p. 98) described "Cactus thickets or shore hammocks" as a widely distributed plant association of the coastal areas of the tip of Florida and the Florida Keys. These cactus thickets are included as an integral part of the Cape Sable hammocks inasmuch as they form an understory in this area; when growing on the marl shores of the Florida Bay keys or on the coral rock of the Florida Keys, however, they may warrant listing as a distinct plant association.

The trees are fast growing, frequently of large diameter but relatively low (30 feet) and topped by the frequent storms. Buttonwood forms a conspicuous component and at times grows in nearly pure stands. Gumbo-limbo, Jamaica dogwood, dove plum, sea grape, wild lime, white and Spanish stoppers, catsclaw, mastic, and saffron plum are common. The Cape Sable hammocks carry one of the richest floras of the Saline Mangrove Zone.

Cape Sable Prairies

The Cape Sable prairies are considered also a distinct plant association. They lie between the beaches and the hammock growth to the rear in three separate, roughly elliptical blocks.

Soil. Over the subsoil is well aerated beach shell and quartz sand formed in low (2.0 to 4.0 feet) dunes by high storm tides. The total depth varies from 8 feet to 12 feet (Craighead and Gilbert, 1962; Craighead, 1964). Between the low ridges, marl is deposited with each hurricane, sealing these troughs to hold seawater or rainwater, depending on the storm tides and amounts of precipitation. Consequently, the plants in these deeper troughs are quite different from those of the ridges. In the days of sailing ships, it was customary to stop for water at Middle Cape, where fresh water was obtained from barrels sunk into these troughs (Simpson, 1923).

Vegetation. Few trees grow on the Cape Sable prairies with the exception of the fire-resistant cabbage and coconut palms and an occasional thatch palm. Scattered Jamaica dogwoods are established. There is a large colony of saw palmetto on Northwest Cape, a coastal remnant of extensive mats of this palm that disappeared with the rising sea. On the banks of the headwater creeks of nearly all the coastal rivers, this plant is still common. Several miles downstream, the remains of prostrate stems can be found in some of the buttonwood hammocks, indicating a rather recent retreat of this species landward. It is believed that these remnants could have lived here 50 years ago prior to the lowering of higher freshwater levels that held the salt water back. Several species of cactus, together with yucca, agave, bay cedar, and sea lavender, are common here. These were torn out by hurricane tides in 1960 and 1965 and were carried to the rear and piled against the hammock growth.

Ponds

In the extensive juncus marshes between the estuaries, ponds are numerous; there are also many ponds in the

Mangrove ponds. *Mangrove ponds are numerous in the mangrove flats, juncus swamps, and saw grass marshes. They are gradually filling with mud and peat to form a continuous soil surface as the red mangroves, juncus, or sedges on the perimeter push inward. The mud is soft and soupy; it extends to bedrock 4 to 10 feet below, but long-legged birds can wade on it when the ponds are full of water. When dry, the mud lies only a few inches below the general land surface level, about one-half to 1 foot mean sea level. When the pond surface is thoroughly dry it will support a man's weight. Cabbage palms are disappearing in the saline mangrove swamps, probably due to increased salinity. Most of the trees in this area, just south of Onion Key, are dead or dying.*

mangrove flats. All are an important feature of the Saline Mangrove Zone. Ponds are considered to be remnants of former open water areas that have not been completely filled as the surrounding marl and peat built up. These areas are now gradually filling, contracting in size, and are being obliterated by several processes, depending on the surrounding vegetation and distance from the seashore.

In the saline zone, the ponds are usually filled with a soupy mud and peat mixture that does not support weight when flooded. Often a soil auger, if held upright, will sink to bedrock 6 to 10 feet below. When dry, however, this mud solidifies and will support one's weight in walking across the surface. The surface of this dry mud in the center of the pond is usually about 0.5 to 1.5 feet below mean sea level. The mud in these outer ponds appears to be a mixture of marl and finely divided red mangrove peat from hurricane deposits. It is of fine texture, apparently the material that Davis (1940) and Spackman et al. (1966) described as "liver mud."

The surface water in these ponds is either fresh or saline, depending on the most recent source, rainfall or tide. The muds are always saline (2,000 to 10,000 ppm.) There is

Mrazek Pond. *During the rainy season when these ponds are filled with fresh water and the surrounding swamps are flooded, the shallow, coffee-colored water is rich in food materials. They support tremendous populations of small invertebrates and fish. As the water disappears through evapotranspiration, the animal life becomes concentrated in the ponds, which literally become almost solid with living organisms. Then great numbers of birds collect to feed.*

Mrazek Pond. *During the last few days of drying out as many as 25 species of birds can be seen feeding in the ponds. The ducks and long-legged birds come first, and those with shorter legs follow as the water depth decreases. After the last morsel of food was consumed, alligators moved across this pond to deeper waters and better hunting grounds.*

little or no vegetation in the smaller ponds, but those of one-fourth acre or more contain less mud, the water is less turbid, and they often contain considerable ruppia, naias, and chara. Some of these larger, deeper ponds had large populations of bigmouth bass and bream prior to Hurricane Donna. Most of these have restocked following several wet years, particularly in 1969.

Many of the ponds are surrounded by red mangrove, which is advancing and replacing the marl (Craighead, 1964) with a compact, red mangrove peat under the plants. Thus, some ponds are gradually contracting and disappearing by this process.

Other ponds with firmer mud were suddenly populated with red and white mangrove seeds and seedlings by Hurricane Donna. The maturation of all three mangrove seeds coincides with the height of the hurricane season—late August and throughout September. Three years later some ponds carried a solid stand of saplings 3 to 6 feet tall. The topsoil becomes firmed in the mass of roots, forming a surface sufficient to support one's weight. Beneath this surface, however, the soil still remained soupy in samples obtained with a coring device.

A third process of stabilization of the muddy surface was observed in the mixed juncus and saw grass marshes farther inland. These two plants pushed into the pond to form a firm sod, 4 to 6 inches thick, that floated upon the unstable watery muck. Often cattails play a prominent role, forming a perimeter of vegetation.

Many ponds of the freshwater area just inland to the Buttonwood Levee are also unfilled holes in the slowly rising land mass. At places they are so numerous that the land and water surfaces appear to be about equal, as just north of West and Cuthbert lakes. These waters are shallower, rarely over 4 feet deep, and, as a rule, they contain less mud in proportion to the water they hold. They

Freshwater pond in the higher rocky glades. *This freshwater pond is at the edge of the pinelands near Culvert 32. It is a large solution hole with an underground cave in the limestone. Ten years ago it was a favored alligator site. A marl bottom retains water long after the surrounding glades are dry. Since 1961, however, this pond, which normally held 6 feet of water, completely dries out each year due to the lengthened dry season resulting from the lowered water table of all of the Park area east of the Shark River Slough and north of the Buttonwood Embankment. The thousands of shallow ponds in the higher glades and pineland no longer develop populations of food fishes. Even in the deeper gator holes where fish can reproduce, they die prematurely as the oxygen supply is depleted. That such an extensive area no longer can support the food chain, and the fact that the water is too deep in the Shark River Slough to make food available, has lowered the productivity of the rookeries over the past few years and driven all land-inhabiting creatures from the dying tree islands of the Everglades slough. Even the alligators cannot feed normally and have few places to nest or bask. Man's mismanagement has destroyed in a few years what natural forces maintained for over 5,000 years.*

are much richer in plant and animal life, harboring some ten species of small food fishes, bream, bigmouth bass, gar, mudfish, and occasionally marine fishes such as tarpon, redfish, and snook. The latter may come in with hurricane tides. Red mangrove forms the banks of many of them. These are now closing rapidly. Those surrounded by higher banks forested with buttonwood, coco plum, red bay, and myrtle appear to be more stable. Alligators were once numerous and played a role in keeping the freshwater ponds cleared of vegetation.

Mangrove Flats

The finest stands of mangroves are all inland to the coastal levee and prairies, along the banks of the larger rivers, and on the numerous islands or inland flats with tidal connections. Here on deep soils 6 to 10 feet in thickness these trees reach their maximum growth. (See pp. 12, 13, 14, 15, and 16.)

Characteristic of all these stands is the fact that they grow in slight depressions. This no doubt has suggested the term "mangrove flats" in common usage in this area. The elevation of the surface soil is about 0.3 feet above mean sea level to about 0.3 feet below. Surrounding these flats is a levee of slightly higher ground, a bit above normal high tide but lower than the highest tides. Those flats along the larger rivers may have numerous small breaks that allow the passage of normal tides. Thus the flats trap saline water from unusually high tides, or fresh water from summer rains; consequently, the root systems of these trees are normally flooded. The seedlings cannot stand drought until they are three years old. Prop roots of older red mangroves reach down as much as 5 feet to tap lower water reserves.

The shoreline of the larger islands, such as those at the mouth of the Shark River and in Whitewater Bay, slope gradually upward for 50 to 150 feet inland. Here red mangroves predominate. On the larger islands, such as those between Shark, Broad, Lostman's, and other west coast rivers, the mangrove trees decrease in size toward the interiors of the islands. These interiors are vegetated by juncus, halophytes, grasses, and sedges and are spotted with ponds of various sizes. All evidence points toward the gradual filling of such enclosed ponds and lakes and the building up of new soils from hurricane marl and peat deposits from the marsh plants. The lack of firmness in these interior soils as compared to that of the tough marl and fibrous peat nearer the coast and the larger rivers probably explains the absence of any stands of large mangrove trees. Scattered small trees are numerous.

Soil. The soil under these large trees is 6 to 12 feet in depth. On the river bank elevations, firm mangrove peat forms the first 2 to 3 feet of soil, lying on top of several feet of mucky peat and 1 to 3 feet of humus-stained mud to bedrock. The stained portions have been darkened by the penetration of organic acids and particles of finely divided organic matter. Helisoma shells and saw grass remains attest to the fact that these deeper muds were laid down in fresh water. Along the large rivers and the perimeters of the mangrove islands the soil is often undercut to bedrock. This peat on top is extremely resistant to erosion, but the muds on which it originated are cut away by tides and form the so-called "caves of the fishermen." One such creek is known as Cave Creek.

Vegetation. Very few plants grow under the shade of the mangrove forests. Where the stand is broken the usual halophytes (as described under Batis Marshes, p. 94) are abundant. The mangrove mallow and Christmasberry are found sparingly. Two rubber vines occur, rhabdadenia and urechites. They often climb to the tops of those stands of moderate height.

Scrub Mangrove

This association is readily recognized as a low, almost impenetratable, closely packed mass of stunted red mangrove trees 4 to 6 feet tall. The stems are interwoven, and the prop roots are too high to step over and too low to crawl under. To cross this interwoven tangle of roots and branches requires constant use of a machete. Close examination of the tangled prop roots fails to identify individual trees. The tough peat surface is exposed at mean tide and covered at high tide. It averages about 0.2 to 0.3 feet above

Scrub mangroves. *This association covers many thousands of acres in the estuarine swamps of South Florida. It forms a dense tangle of red mangrove prop roots that are too high to step over and too strong to break through. They have been growing on the same sites for 500 to 2,000 years, building up a tough, firm peat with the slowly rising sea. This peat becomes too dense for the prop roots to penetrate, resulting in the dwarfing of the plants. The creeks here are too deep for the prop roots to reach out and fasten to the muddy bottom. In other places where the flow of water has lessened, mud has filled in, and the prop roots take hold and bridge the open water. Many creeks have thus been closed in the past fifty years. The bleached ghost trees are dead buttonwoods gradually being killed by the rising salt water. On the elevated creek bank in the foreground the buttonwood is still living. Several saline buttonwood tree islands of taller trees are shown here. These trees survive because they occur on elevations of 1 to 1.5 feet.*

mean water level. When this type occurs as much as 5 to 6 miles inland, the surface of the soil retains its same relation to local water levels, which may be several tenths above sea level. This community covers as much area, or more, than that of the mangrove flats.

Soil. The peat soil of this scrub is as characteristic as its aerial growth. It is a very firm, tough mass of prop and feeding roots, so compacted that it is almost impossible to push a coring device through it or even a one-half inch probing rod. It can be cut into blocks with a pointed saw and then removed. It has been named Joe River Peat because of the extensive beds along the river (Llewellyn, 1967).

This firm peat contracts very little on drying. Many of the prop roots slant at various angles or are even horizontal instead of perpendicular, as found in other red mangrove peat. This reddish, fibrous peat grades 2 to 4 feet below the surface into a mucky saw grass peat, or into a freshwater (Helisoma) marl.

The explanation for the stunted growth of this scrub seems to lie in the compacted condition of the peat. A close analogy might be a potbound plant—a natural bonsai tree. It is obvious that the prop roots cannot penetrate deeply into this dense fibrous mass.

Vegetation. The saline scrub mangrove is notably lacking in associated species of plants. Where slightly higher elevations (0.5 feet msl) occur, they are invaded by a few shrubs and ferns characteristic of buttonwood hammocks. Buttonwood, randia, Christmasberry, and the swamp and leather ferns are the most common. Where fresh water floods these swamps during the hydroperiod, several trees appear—mahogany, saffron plum, Spanish stopper, and myrsine—as the community merges into a buttonwood strand or island.

Another type of scrub red mangrove occurs in patches near the coast. In this type the plants are similar to the foregoing in appearance but they are not so densely placed or as tall, rarely over 4 feet. This community is growing on outcrops of mud rock (Ginsberg, 1958). The red mangroves are restricted to pockets in between the round pallets of rock. These rock patties resemble large dinner plates of laminated layers with slightly upcurved edges. The outcrops occur at several places from Black Point to Card Sound and on Big Pine Key.

Juncus Marshes

Throughout the Saline Mangrove Zone there are small juncus swamps of a few acres as well as extensive areas of several square miles. These swamps lie between the main rivers or form the interior of the larger mangrove islands.

Black rush. Juncus roemerianus *forms extensive communities in Province III, the Saline Mangrove Zone. Rarely small patches are found in freshwater areas subject to occasional flooding by hurricane tides. Along the fluctuating line between salt and fresh water, this rush often invades the saw grass swamps, completely replacing the former vegetation. In this illustration, fire destroyed the peaty creek bank, permitting salt waters to flood the saw grass during the dry season, when high winds pushed the tides far inland and gradually destroyed the plants. Some remaining saw grass shows along the bottom of the photographs. Bedrock is 5 to 7 feet beneath, and many former small ponds have gradually filled with mud and peat.*

Like the mangrove flats, they hold salt water part of the year and fresh water during the rainy season.

Soil. The soil profile is 6 to 12 feet in depth, and consists of a dark muck of varying firmness, containing much saw grass peat. It extends downward several feet to meet the freshwater Helisoma muds and the basal freshwater mud lying on bedrock. These sediments reveal a history of extensive saw grass swamps that were overrun by the rising sea and invaded by halophytes. This process is currently active a few miles inland.

Vegetation. Juncus roemerianus predominates in these marshes, but often a salt-tolerant fringe rush *(Fimbristylis castanea)* forms up to 40 percent of the ground cover. Patches of saw grass remain on elevations of over 0.5 feet, as around tree islands. Usually buttonwood islands with their swamp tree associates are spotted within the larger swamps. Here the peat is firmer and of the Gandy type (Henderson, 1939) of hammock peat. The soil profile shows that these peat areas reach to bedrock and have been building up over the past 4,000 years as the sea rose.

Spartina Communities

Five species of spartina are found in the area. The most abundant, *Spartina spartinae,* or prickly cord grass, forms small to large colonies that often cover several hundred acres. Extensive stands are found on the Flamingo prairie and on the flats between the larger estuaries. This species grows in drier areas just above high tide, but frequent storm flooding does not discourage it.

Farther inland near the Buttonwood Embankment, stands of another species, sand cord grass, *S. bakeri,* occupy a considerable area between the estuaries of all the rivers from the Broad River to Naples. Here it grows on land that is sometimes covered with very high tides. Spartina stands and juncus stands alternate on this site, and there is some mixing.

In the freshwater swamps or higher glades north of the Buttonwood Embankment, *S. bakeri* forms scattered colonies. *Fimbristylis castanea* (brown fringe rush) and at times saw grass are also components. This association is reported to be the habitat of the rare Cape Sable Sparrow.

Two of the other species are tidal, *S. cynosurordes* (big cord grass) and *S. alternifolia,* and just above high tide is found *S. patens,* a less abundant species. More study of spartina communities is needed.

River Banks

The river banks of the Saline Mangrove Zone also have been mentioned under mangrove flats. Inasmuch as these sloping and slightly elevated shores escaped the devastation by Hurricane Donna (Craighead, 1964), it seems desirable to call attention to them as a distinct association. The hurricane immunity seems to have resulted from the fact that the ebb and flow of the tides washed the mud deposits from these shores. Furthermore, the soil is a deep, firm, red mangrove peat, and the vegetation is chiefly red mangrove plus the common halophytes where the stands are open. Upstream where the fresh and tidal waters merge, the river banks become slightly more elevated and buttonwood becomes the dominant tree among the red and white mangroves. At many places buttonwood forms long strands, marking the original river bank (possibly 3,000 years old). Often these strands are from 50 to 300 yards inland of the scrub mangrove forest that has built outward gradually, narrowing the rivers.

Farther upstream many other swamp hardwoods come in as the transition to freshwater creeks becomes more pronounced. These are randia, saffron plum, poisonwood, mahogany, white stopper, and wax myrtle.

Vegetation. Three vines are conspicuous on the river banks from their estuary mouths to the freshwater creeks. Two of these, *Rhabdadenia biflora* (rubber vine) and *Erechites lutea* (wild allamanda), both belonging to the family Apocynacae, are called "rubber vines" because of their milky juice. They have tough, rope-like stems that climb to 20 feet or so with hanging profusions of white or yellow flowers. Erechites is found in brackish to fresh water, and rhabdadenia often sends long runners diagonally across a creek to climb to sunlight on the far bank. These tough ropes collect quantities of debris and branches in the slowly moving currents.

The third vine is the moonflower, *Calonyction aculeatum,* which grows in great profusion not only in the Saline Mangrove Zone wherever it can find the slightest rise above high tide but far inland wherever woody plants are found. Great masses of large, white, salver-shaped flowers appear every evening and disappear at sunrise. They climb to the tallest hammock trees and cling tenaciously for years, suppressing tree growth. In the pineland hammocks they appear wanting unless one is able to recognize the slender woody lianas hanging from the treetops. A better way to see them is on an early morning airplane flight when they can be recognized as white floral patches capping the canopies of large mastic or lysiloma trees.

PROVINCE IV – FRESHWATER SWAMPS

This province lies landward to the tidal areas. It is a large, shallow, crescent-shaped area of fresh water impounded behind the Buttonwood Embankment. During the rainy season the Freshwater Swamps are filled with water to an elevation of about 1.5 feet mean sea level, at which height they begin to overflow the Buttonwood Embankment. These waters extend inland, sloping with the land, to the edge of the pineland, where the elevation of the glade soil is about 1.5 feet at the extreme southern end, or farther north to higher land of 3 or 4 feet. The soil surface may then at times be covered with 1 foot of water sloping with the land. Leveling off is retarded by the vegetation.

Much peaty material has built up in these mangrove Freshwater Swamps where the waters remain most of the year, chiefly just inside the embankment. At some places this deposit has extended inland 3 miles or so to form extensive spongy beds of organic matter. Numerous tree islands dot the landscape. Between these, where the bedrock is deepest in basins, solution holes, and sloughs, saw grass is found growing on deep (2.0 to 5.0 feet) beds of peat. Where the soil is shallow marl 0.5 to 1.0 feet deep, spike rush is the dominant plant.

Geology and Hydrology

The bedrock is of Miami or Bryozoan limestone in Dade County east of the Shark River, and of Tamiami limestone of the Miocene period in Collier and Monroe counties west of the Shark. Variations of bedrock are from minus 5.0 to plus 4.0 feet. At several places in western Dade and Monroe counties a find sand underlies the overburden of peat. This has been referred to as the Anastasia formation.

Fresh water 2 to 3 feet deep lies just inside the Buttonwood Levee, becoming shallower inland to where it often remains dry during late winter and spring. This water

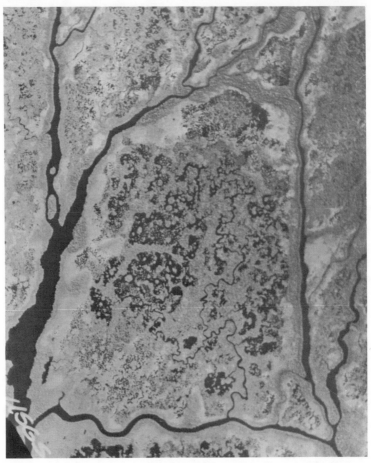

The Apex. *This U.S. Geological Survey photograph illustrates the intricate pattern of plant communities in transition areas between saline and fresh water. The area shown covers about 1 by 1.5 miles near the junction of the North (left) and Roberts (right) rivers. Here saline and fresh water alternate with the dry and rainy seasons.*

The lightest areas represent juncus and transition to red mangrove; light gray areas are saw grass, often mixed with red mangrove; dark gray circular patches are buttonwood islands and strands; black areas indicate creeks and ponds; closing creeks can be seen at the lower left and top left of this photograph.

In this area the overburden on the bedrock is 3 to 7 feet deep. The ponds are shallower, and the bay heads and red mangroves deepest. Raised river banks (white line on left bank of Roberts River) carry buttonwood overtopping the margin of red mangrove (for detail, see p. 121). The river embankment has been destroyed by fire (middle of photo, right bank) after which salt water invaded the saw grass, which is now (light patch) replaced by juncus. (opposite).

is largely supplied by rainfall, but there is a considerable flow from the Shark River Slough, the higher pinelands, and the Big Cypress farther inland (in Monroe and Collier counties). Considerable water may possibly arise in spring-like seepages from the bedrock.

Soils

The calcitic mud soils are formed in fresh water and are rarely more than 4.0 feet in thickness near the Buttonwood Embankment. They thin gradually inland to where the bedrock outcrops. These marl soils are broken by pockets of red mangrove peat near the Buttonwood Levee and more extensive beds of saw grass peat farther inland. In many places the soil profile is stratified with alternating beds of saw grass peat and marl; these are interpreted to represent a series of wet years when peat was preserved, and a series of

Closing creeks. *In the brackish swamps, many creeks have closed with the decreasing flow of water over the last 50 years, even though the sea is gradually rising. As the head of fresh water decreases, mud builds up in the creeks. When the mud nears about 18 inches of the surface, the ever-reaching red mangrove prop roots take hold, debris accumulates, and gradually the creek is blocked. Some of the creeks that were passable to canoes in 1952 are now closed. The once-abundant alligators also played an important role in keeping such creeks open.*

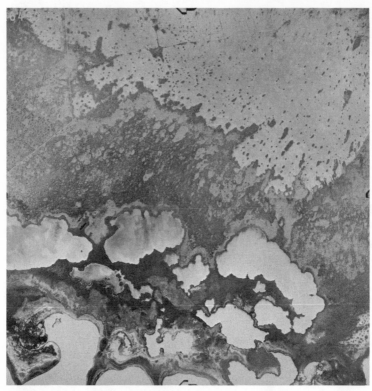

West Lake Area. *The area illustrated here is north of Florida Bay, and is some 15 miles long and 10 miles wide. The three large lakes, West, Cuthbert, and Seven Palm, vary from fresh in the rainy season to brackish in the winter. Two tidal creeks enter from Florida Bay. North of these lakes are the shallow Freshwater Swamps of Province IV. The Buttonwood Embankment north of the three lakes formed at the landward edge of the Saline Mangrove Zone. It is about 1.5 feet above the mean water level of the lakes and is 100 to 200 yards wide. It serves as a levee impounding the freshwater glades to the north. It continues across the Park, broken in places, on the inner bank of the string of lakes and bays, and along the small tributaries pushing into the saw grass of the Freshwater Swamps. A saw grass swamp lies just inland to this levee, and beyond that, a block of recently closing ponds and vegetation that includes red mangrove clumps, patches of saw grass, bay heads, cypress domes, and much buttonwood. These are gradually building up peat and replacing the saw grass and filling in the ponds. In time, lacking fires in the saw grass, this will be a solid stand of red mangroves and swamp hardwoods. This recent buildup of peat and vegetation is explained by the deeper (3 to 6 feet) bedrock of this area and the consequent longer retention of water in the dry season.*

Just north of this dense vegetation is a shallow, light-colored area (1 to 1.5 feet msl) where 6 to 18 inches of marl support a spike rush swamp. This swamp is spotted with many beautiful tree islands growing on small mesas and in depressions in the bedrock. *This slightly higher land is frequently dry in the winter.*

To the top of the photograph a rock reef extends northeast for 9 miles. This has been completely broken down by dissolution from beneath, and the trough has been largely replaced by red mangroves and buttonwood. It is known as Whiskey Creek. The remains of more than 20 stills have been found on these islands, indicating a once-flourishing industry. The light area north of Whiskey Creek is a spike rush community, with patches of saw grass swamps in the deeper basins. Here small rock mesas, remains of earlier erosion, are forested with tropical hardwoods. These elevated areas are called hammocks. In addition, many buttonwood strands, bay heads, willow heads, and cypress heads are scattered about. Moats, well stocked with largemouth bass, surround the bay heads. Formerly this area supported a large population of alligators and provided a rich feeding ground for wading birds. Otters were once abundant. A few sandhill cranes are sometimes still seen here.

Detail of creek bank. *This photograph shows a red mangrove fringe remaining at the water's edge. The tall buttonwoods have suppressed the mangroves beneath them. No prop roots show in this picture because of the water depth of 5 to 6 feet.*

Physiographic Provinces and Plant Associations 121

Land-building north of West Lake. *The light and gray patches are ponds 3 to 4 feet deep, often 6 feet to bedrock, partly filled with soupy mud formed by periphyton (the lightest patches). The gray patches are open ponds filled with bladderwort and other submerged plants. The woody plants, chiefly red mangrove, buttonwood, and red bay, have become established where the marl has reached the surface. Here Gandy peat is laid down. Soil profiles show stratification of alternating marl and peat beds. This indicates that past fires that destroyed the vegetation in periods of drought and subsequent periods of flooding were features of the past 3,000 years.*

dry years when the land surface dried, as has been the case for the past twenty years. This marl is deposited by the periphyton.

Vegetation

The flora of this province is varied. Near the embankment it is composed of red and white mangroves or saw grass marshes. Inland, numerous bay heads are present, forested with freshwater swamp trees that can endure an occasional inundation by hurricane tides.

Saw grass patches and sloughs are abundant in depressions of the bedrock. Several species of spike rushes and beak rushes are common on the marl soils. Still farther inland near the edge of hurricane tides, cypress and willow heads are numerous.

Plant Associations

Sixteen principal plant associations will be described; they are: Red and White Mangrove Swamps; Tree Islands; Buttonwood Strands and Islands; Bay Heads; Tropical Hardwood Hammocks; Saw Palmetto Rings; Palm Savannas; Cypress Domes and Strands; Willow Heads; Pop Ash Heads; Custard Apple Swamps; Saw Grass Marshes; Spike Rush Marshes; Ponds; Creek Banks; and Casaurina and Other Exotics.

Red and White Mangrove Swamps

The transition from the Saline Mangrove Zone to the Freshwater Swamps and their mangrove communities may be gradual or well defined. The line of demarkation is vague where the Buttonwood Embankment has been destroyed by fire and sharp where the levee is well preserved.

This association covers an extensive area within the freshwater zone in the Park. Salt water encroaches over much of its entire breadth during severe hurricanes and also when high southwesterly winds and dry glades coincide. These tides during September bring all three species of mangrove seeds into the area, but only the red and white become established as the water recedes. Along the deeper soils near the embankment where the soil is 2 or 4 feet deep, these trees coalesce to form a complete ground cover. Farther inland, the white drops out and the red forms low red mangrove clumps, or "spiders," 3 to 6 feet tall, rooted in the numerous solution holes of the bedrock. These clumps are widely scattered inland. Only in occasional places in the deeper sinks have they developed to heights of 25 or 30 feet. Two factors seem to be predominant in this: neither tree can stand a dry soil, and each is highly susceptible to fire. Before the Park was established, fires occurred frequently in the saw grass communities of this association.

Soil. A layer of peat underlies the mangrove clumps. It is variable in depth, at times replacing the marl to bedrock in the solution holes. Many of the living clumps are probably over 100 years of age. Little observable growth has occurred in the past fifteen years or more. Often the soil is stratified with marl and freshwater shell, apparently representing dry periods when the mangrove clumps were destroyed by fire. These, unfortunately, have not been dated. They probably represent periods of relatively wet years when saw grass was abundant and dry years when the periphyton was dominant. Most of the present soil surface between clumps is gray marl covered with periphyton during the months of the hydro-period.

Freshwater red and white mangrove swamps. *These swamps are locally called dwarf mangroves or red mangrove spiders. The red mangrove seedlings and to some extent the seeds of the white mangrove drift inland as much as 10 miles into the freshwater swamps. Several large patches of red mangrove occur more than 15 miles inland in the Shark River Slough, and a colony exists near the Anhinga Trail. A buttonwood strand forms the background of this photograph. As the seedlings drift inward, driven on high waters by strong winds, they become established generally over the area but survive only in a scattered pattern. Only those seedlings that come to rest over a solution hole in the bedrock can survive. Here the roots can reach down to water 2 feet or so below in the dry seasons. Seedlings by the thousands that are not so fortunate die each dry season. As the sea gradually rises over these almost level lands, the inland fresh waters become relatively deeper in relation to the bedrock, the pioneer clumps gradually coalesce, and the peat beds thicken. The new trees increase in height and a forest cover is established.*

Closeup of red mangroves established in a solution hole. *Two 4-foot lathes were pushed to bedrock, one in the solution hole and the other just outside, to illustrate the survival of the mangrove clumps in solution holes.*

Vegetation. Where the mangroves coalesce into a solid cover, few other plants are present. Several epiphytic bromeliads and orchids occur. At places these festoon the hosts, giving a distinctive character to the "spiders." The glade marl between the scattered mangrove spiders is occupied by a number of plants. Among these are several sedges and grasses, saw grass, horned beak rush, spike rush, maiden cane, manisurus, plume grass, *Spartina bakeri,* reed, cattails, arrowheads, and burreed. The common epiphytes are yellow catopsis, twisted airplant, reddish wild pine, ball moss, dollar orchid, and butterfly orchid.

Tree Islands

Tree islands will be discussed in general before designating their division into several distinct plant associations that compose the arborescent vegetation of the Freshwater Swamps. All types of tree islands stand out in sharp contrast to the surrounding glade communities. Each has distinct characteristics.

Included under the term "tree islands" are hammocks,

bay heads, willow heads, cypress strands and domes, buttonwood strands and domes, custard apple swamps, and pop ash heads. Tree islands occur in several plant associations from the high rock land of the pinelands to the saline marshes. One common characteristic is that they are all supported on a base of organic soil. In the case of hammocks, the Gandy peat soil lies on a slight rock mesa 1 to 5 feet above the surrounding level. Thus the roots are well aerated for the greater part of the year. In the bay heads, on the other hand, the organic soil is usually built up above the usual water level. Cypress heads, willow heads, and pop ash heads have little or no buildup of peat above the usual high water. Abrupt flooding held for several months will destroy all types of tree islands.

There is some transition from one type to another as the elevation of the soil builds up or is degraded. Fire plays a major role in the evolution of these communities. Normally none of the tree islands are seriously injured by fire, as the organic soil is quite moisture-retentive. In drought periods, however, when the moisture content of the peat or mucky soil beneath them dries to below 25 percent, it is possible for them to be completely burned out. All plants may be destroyed, leaving a rocky mesa in the case of a hammock or rocky basins of various depths.

The shapes of these tree islands are variable. In the Shark River Slough they are long and lenticular. In the less watery areas of the Everglades they tend to be more oval, or may take the form of perfect circles. Some have long "tails" of saw grass, willow, or other tall vegetation, usually downstream, but often one to three additional tails may project in another direction. Considerable speculation relating to the shapes of these hammocks and the meaning of their tails is found in the literature (Davis, 1943; Loveless, 1959). It has been suggested that the "grain" of these tree islands follows the direction of the drainage pattern (Fig. 5). In the area north of Florida Bay, the circular form is more prevalent. The circular form is characteristic of many plant islands, especially those made of sedges, grasses, and mangroves, when they expand naturally without the pressure of other forces. The tails, likewise no doubt indicate a long-continued drainage pattern, such as that of the Shark

River Slough. In other places the tree islands may have 2 to 5 tails. These tails, on probing, are found to be growing in deep furrows of the bedrock and seem to be one of the "legs" of the spider-like erosion pattern formed when the limestone was relatively higher in relation to the sea level. If this reasoning is sound, it offers evidence of variations in the drainage patterns of the recent past since the limestone became exposed.

Buttonwood Strands and Islands

Buttonwood associations have quite a different character in the Freshwater Swamps from those in the Saline Mangrove Zone. Here on the more calcareous soils, the buttonwood trees form a much larger proportion of the arborescent vegetation, although the trees themselves are not as large. This is particularly true along the embankments bordering the lakes and bays that cross the Park and on the banks of many tributaries.

Buttonwood, red mangrove, and saw grass are pioneer species in these glades, colonizing the calcitic mudbanks formed by the floating periphyton and wind drift (Craighead, 1964). These floating seeds occupy mudbanks soon after a slight recession of the glade waters exposes the surface of the mud and permits seeds to lodge. Once the seedlings are established on these low embankments, grasses, sedges, coco plum, and several swamp hardwoods follow. Buttonwood usually remains the dominant tree, however, and it characterizes the strands that may extend for several miles. These buttonwood strands are numerous and impound or slow down the flow of water. Along with the rock reefs they are an important factor in the drainage system of the Park.

Soil. The soil of this plant association is chiefly a shallow marl base on bedrock, usually less than 2 feet deep. This is usually capped by 6 to 18 inches of hammock peat. When these islands overlay deep basins, however, 6 to 8 feet of hammock peat may extend to bedrock, indicating considerable age, 3,000 years or more.

Vegetation. The plants of freshwater buttonwood strands are quite similar to those of the bay heads. The more open character of these strands permits a great amount of saw grass to grow on the humus floor beneath the buttonwood trees. Often it forms a solid ground cover, 5 to 6 feet high, or it may occur as tufts on slight elevations if the hammock surface is low. Coco plum is also a common component of these strands, sometimes forming a solid understory. More often it is overtopped by buttonwood and crowded to the perimeter with red mangrove. Both coco plum and buttonwood are very susceptible to frost and become less dominant inland.

Swamp fern and both species of leather ferns may form much of the ground cover. Epiphytes are abundant, both bromeliads and orchids. The vine orchid occurs commonly. Two other large vines, dalbergia and hippocratea, are also present.

Bay Heads

Bay heads are tree islands composed of swamp hardwoods growing on elevations of gandy peat; in this area these may vary from 1 to 4 feet in height above the surrounding marsh. Bay heads are typical of all the freshwater areas excepting the pinelands but are best developed in the lower portions where water remains longer. These islands are usually dome-shaped, but when quite large (up to 25 acres or more) may be flat-topped or have a strandlike appearance.

Most bay heads originate in solution holes or basins in the bedrock where water is retained and, consequently, where peat accumulates. The depth to bedrock is often 4 or 5 feet and may even be as much as 8 feet near the saline mangroves. Some bay heads, however, undoubtedly have replaced former burned-out hammocks. In some of these the limestone prominences may be slightly above the glade level, usually pinnacled with deep recesses. Thus a profile across such tree islands shows both high rock and deep solution holes.

Another characteristic feature of tree islands of marshy areas is the presence of a shallow moat, 10 to 20 feet wide, around their perimeters (Small, 1933). A red mangrove ring surrounds the island and forms an inner edge of this moat. Typically, the marl soil in this moat is shallower than in the

Bay heads. *The most common type of tree island is probably the bay head. They occur in great numbers completely around the three-county area just inside the Saline Mangrove Zone. In most cases the peaty soil is built up 1 to 3 feet above the general ground level. Usually bay heads are surrounded by a shallow moat inhabited by alligators and fishes. Hurricanes bring in seawater to cover many of them for a few days. Most of the vegetation is tolerant to part-time flooding, but it will be destroyed if the roots are covered throughout the year and cannot be properly aerated.*

surrounding glade. Only 2 to 4 inches may be present near its inner edge among the mangrove roots, while beyond in the glade land it may be 12 inches in depth.

The moats are strikingly distinct from the air. Usually the marl surface is quite dark and covered by much loose leaf litter, in contrast to the light colored marl of the glade. Little or no periphyton grows here. The explanation for this is not clear. It may be partly the result of the activity of the formerly abundant alligators. The organic acids leaching from the island surface may cause the dissolution of the marl. Again, the shaded perimeter from the overhanging tree island would discourage the growth of the periphyton that precipitates the calcite.

Soil. The soil of the bay heads is almost entirely hammock or Gandy peat. The top is fairly friable and loamy. It carries many small pieces of woody materials in the upper layers (Davis, 1940). The deeper layers become more and more compacted and mucky as they age and integrate with the freshwater marl. Plant material is highly decomposed in the lower levels. A layer of dark marl often lies on the bedrock. In the deeper pockets that penetrate the bedrock, remains of red mangrove peat are frequently found.

Vegetation. The arborescent flora consists chiefly of coco plum, myrica, pigeon plum, buttonwood, red bay, dahoon holly, poisonwood, and sweet bay. In the southern portions of the area, red mangrove and paurotis palm are frequent components. Bromeliads and epiphytic orchids are abundant. Swamp fern usually covers the ground, and leather ferns are common. Saw grass is often tall and composes a luxuriant understory on many of the less elevated bayheads; on the higher peat areas, bracken fern abounds.

Tropical Hardwood Hammocks

This community is fairly common toward the inland border of the province where the bedrock is near the surface or exposed. These hammocks are always on a slight elevation (1 to 4 feet) of the bedrock; these are small mesas that resisted the erosion of the glade. They are essentially similar to the hammocks of the pineland described under Province V, Pineland Ridge.

Saw Palmetto Rings

Where fires have been frequent in the hammock area

Saw palmetto rings. *Numerous, nearly perfect rings of saw palmetto may be seen on the higher glades where the Freshwater Swamps meet the Pineland Ridge. These rings are the remains of former tropical hardwood hammocks that have been destroyed by fires. The sun-loving palmettos keep pushing out to the edge of the hammock, but are quite fire resistant and so survive.*

described above, perfect circles of saw palmetto from 50 to several hundred feet in diameter are found. These have resulted from the complete destruction, by repeated fires, of the arborescent flora of the hammock, leaving the fire-resistant, light-demanding palms that frame the perimeter of the hammock relatively unharmed (Craighead, 1970).

Palm Savannas

Harper (1927) described this community as a prominent vegetative type of south-central Florida, chiefly north of these three southern counties. He also mentions similar associations in Pinellas and Lee counties and remarks that obvious differences in this vegetation in widely separated areas might warrant separate treatment.

On the west coast of Lee and Collier counties, palm patches on sand flats or saw grass marshes present a most picturesque and delightful landscape. Similar communities are found on Cape Sable and on both marl prairies and

Palm savannas. *The cabbage palm is widely distributed in both saline and freshwater areas. However, it cannot survive tidal inundation for any lengthy period. Clumps of cabbage palm are frequent on slightly elevated land in the Saline Mangrove Zone. Many of these are disappearing with the rising sea. In the freshwater areas, this palm is quite abundant, often forming large communities. Light fires that kill invading hardwoods have encouraged pure stands in the savannas.*

brackish swamps in Province III, the Saline Mangrove Zone. Undoubtedly, the life histories of these communities are quite different and deserve separate rank. On Hog Island and the Raulerson Prairie the palmettos are rapidly dying or are completely killed. The rather limited observations by the writer have offered no satisfactory explanation for these deadenings. This problem as well as more study of the palmetto associations is needed.

Cypress Domes and Strands

Cypress domes, heads, or strands, as they are variously called, usually occur in depressions of the bedrock or, if the limestone bedrock is exposed, it is much broken into numerous pinnacles interspersed with deep crevices. The basin-like contours or the irregular pinnacle rock and crevice pattern of these cypress heads are often fully exposed after severe fires that consume all of the organic matter.

Cypress heads in this area usually have a central pond surrounded by the tallest trees of the group. This is especially characteristic of younger stands that have become reestablished since the fires of twenty-five to fifty years ago. No mature cypress heads have been found in the Park proper. Cypress strands are similar except that they follow sloughs where the bedrock has been eroded away to form troughs extending a few hundred yards to several miles in length.

The domed character of these cypress heads has intrigued several writers into suggesting explanations for their distinctive shapes (Harper, 1927; Small, 1931a, 1933; Vernon, 1947; Craighead, 1964). In the three southern counties of Florida where cypress grows in depressions in the limestone bedrock and in a medium with a pH usually about 7.0, the simplest explanation seems to be a difference in site quality. If the rings of the cypress trees in this area represent annual growth, as they seem to do, there is little difference in the age of the tallest trees in the deepest soil and the peripheral trees on shallow soil. In fact, those trees growing on the very shallow soil (2 to 6 inches) are often much older in terms of ring numbers as they are more resistant to fire in those very dry years when the deep peat burns and the domes are destroyed. In other words, the taller trees grow

Cypress domes. *Cypress is one of the most abundant trees of this area. It covers most of Collier and western Monroe counties, and extends in a wide, curving band eastward across the Park to Highway U.S. 1. Here the low, flat land with its numerous depressions and sloughs that once carried water much of the year furnish the necessary requirements for the establishment and growth of this tree. It was much more abundant 50 years ago. Now, few stands within the Park are over 35 years of age and seldom are more than 6 inches in diameter. Around 1937, fires swept much of the cypress belt in the Park, burning out the deep peat. When this happened the trees were killed. A few large trees escaped, and one 5 feet in diameter is still alive. Most of these sites come back, after fires, to cypress. Now with an increasingly lower water table in the eastern part of the belt, the seedlings cannot survive, and swamp hardwoods (as shown in this photograph) are replacing the cypress. Very few of the cypress stands burned out in the extensive fires of 1962 are regenerating to cypress.*

on better sites. The deep peat in the basins is highly fertile, while the perimeter of thin marl is relatively sterile, especially where frequent fires destroy the slight accumulation of organic matter. The dome-like outline fairly well mirrors the contours of the depression (Craighead, 1964).

Cypress in South Florida grows naturally only where water is retained on the surface of the soil for the greater part of the year. Demaree (1932) and Small (1931a) have pointed out that a cypress seed must lodge on bare soil to germinate, but after the seedling begins growth it cannot endure drying. Observations of first-year seedlings 12 to 18 inches tall in Dade County in 1962 and 1965 indicated that all died on two study plots during the prolonged low water table of those years.

Cypress grows quite rapidly on the inner edge of the

Dwarf cypress. *Some of the most attractive plant communities in the area are formed by dwarf cypress. The trees are scattered, growing on thin marl soil 3 to 6 inches deep, which usually has no surface water in the late winter season but is wet the remainder of the year. Seedlings become established in wet years but grow very slowly on the poor sites. Consequently, many small trees are over 100 years of age, while in nearby cypress heads trees of the same size may be only 25 years old. In winter after the leaves fall, scrub cypress stands give a weird grayish, smoky color to the landscape. Many trees assume strange forms and are often spoken of as "ghost" trees and "ghost" forests.*

freshwater marshes. Trees forming the present stands on sites burned out in 1945 are 25 to 30 feet tall and up to 4 inches in diameter (the latter is usually expressed by the forestry term D.B.H., or diameter breast height). Older stands originating after fires of 1930 are 35 to 40 feet tall, with diameters of 6 inches and occasionally up to 8 inches.

Soil. The soil of the cypress domes or sloughs is usually not built up above mean water level except for alligator nests or the mounds over alligator caves. The depth ranges from 1.5 to 6.0 feet deep in this area. It is a dark mucky peat underlaid with darkly stained marl resting on the bedrock.

Vegetation. Cypress domes and sloughs, when fully stocked, are often well shaded and consequently may have very few associated species except such shade-loving plants as the bromeliads, orchids, ferns, and nettles. Most of the marsh-inhabiting shrubs and trees are found in the perimeter; these include buttonwood, red bay, sweet bay, magnolia, coco plum, dahoon holly, myrsine, wax myrtle, willow, and poisonwood. These may increase and build up a thick layer of hardwood peat with the gradual reduction of the cypress in older stands that are in time transformed into bay heads. Numerous dead cypress snags and stumps—some of the latter very large—are present in such cases. In such transition types, tall, vigorous saw grass may be an important component on the higher peat. Occasionally palmettos are present. Greenbriar *(Smilax laurifolia)* is a conspicuous component, climbing high into the trees.

Herbaceous plants include maiden cane, spike rush, pluchea, eupatorium, chloris, swamp fern, and two species of leather fern. Red mangrove occurs in many of these cypress heads, sometimes spreading over much of the perimeter area. Occasionally these red mangroves will form large domes with only a few scattered cypress trees in the stand. Some of these are 18 miles from the coast.

In western Monroe and Collier counties in the sandy limestone potholes, pine is regularly mixed with cypress, the former occupying the slightly higher ground. Cabbage palm is also a common component of these cypress stands.

Willow Heads

Willow heads are strictly a freshwater association. These tree islands are abundant inland and, like cypress domes, may occur in association with red mangroves. Neither willow nor cypress can withstand the flooding of hurricane tides. Willow heads are circular or oval and sometimes form strands. Often an atoll-like rim of firmer soil surrounds a central pond.

To become established, willow requires a disturbed soil on low land subject to part-time flooding. It is intolerant of shade. These conditions are met after fires, in the agricultural activities in the glades, on the fresh soil piled up around gator holes, and in places of erosion. The small plumose seeds are windblown for long distances and also float readily.

Early attempts with agriculture in Dade County were on

Willow heads. *These bright green domes are scattered throughout the area just landward of the highest saline storm tides. They are intolerant of salt water. They once formed the homes of the millions of alligators that inhabited the area, and through the activities of this reptile supplied a habitat that in turn supported much of the area's wildlife. Willow seeds blow about and germinate on disturbed soil that remains moist and from which the roots can reach water throughout the year. The trees grow rapidly where there is ample water, the taller ones on the deeper soils. They seldom spread out into the marl-covered glades unless after a disturbance such as a fire or the clearing of land for agriculture. The numerous solution holes throughout the limestone country offer ideal sites for willow. Even in the higher pinelands, any sink hole that holds water will be colonized by willow. Willow has been extensively killed by the recent flooding of Conservation Area 3.*

the glade land, the sloughs transversing the pineland, and in the glades east of Homestead and Florida City. Most of this land was gradually abandoned, and many of these fields are now nearly pure stands of willow and saltbush mixed with other shrubs. They are quite dense, 15 to 25 feet tall, with large willows reaching 5 to 7 inches in diameter. They have their maximum growth and are now breaking up from the attacks of a stem borer *(Prionoxystus robiniae)* and storms. Willow has increased tremendously in recent years as the result of fire and agricultural activity. In the Shark River Slough it has taken over much of the soil formerly supporting saw grass, and it has replaced other swamp tree species in the bay heads of the slough.

Willow is a common associate of the cypress heads and the more inland mangrove clumps. Willow heads form around large solution holes, basins, or sloughs that hold water for much of the year. They are usually deep, 4 to 6 feet—and some even 10 feet—where the roots can reach water during the driest periods. In these places the trees rarely are more than 15 feet tall. More commonly, however, they are broken and more or less prostrate, with the bases still living and putting out new suckers.

The breakage is a result of an almost 100 percent infestation by the larvae of the previously mentioned wood borer. The larvae extensively tunnel the wood, making it readily subject to windthrow. This borer seems to control the height of the willow clumps.

Willow heads are one of the most favored habitats of alligators and they, in turn, do much to maintain the depressions, which otherwise would quickly fill with organic matter and be replaced by herbaceous and woody swamp hardwoods. The depressions abound in fish and are a most important factor in wildlife survival (Craighead, 1968).

Soil. The soil of the willow heads is not very firm. In the ponds it is composed chiefly of a mucky peat, a mixture of dark, disintegrated plant remains and marl. This is often of a soupy consistency of fine, organic matter that is difficult to hold in a coring device used for soil sampling. The rim surrounding the central pond is a more firm, Gandy peat. When these holes fill with water, a probe will sink to near bedrock by its own weight, but when dry the surface is only about 1 to 1.5 feet below the high water level. Then the material is firm enough to walk across. The deepest muck in these ponds is of a black, plastic consistency. When air-dried it becomes very hard, so much so that it requires a hammer to break it. Coal geologists who have examined the material state that it resembles the brown coal of Germany (Smith, personal communication, 1964).

Vegetation. The principal arborescent plants of the willow heads are pond apple, willow, red bay, sweet bay, wax myrtle, cypress, buttonbush, coco plum, holly, buttonwood, and poisonwood.

Saw grass is abundant and best developed on the slightly higher ground. Other herbaceous vegetation is chiefly composed of the following species: ribbon lily, pickerelweed, green arum, spilanthes, septate bulrush, great bulrush, three-square maiden cane, spider lily, arrowhead, water purslane, matted figwort, and aromatic figwort.

Pop Ash Heads

Pop ash is a common swamp tree of the western portions of Monroe and Collier counties. It occurs with cypress and several swamp hardwoods, and frequently it is found in pure stands of one-tenth to several acres. These communities are essentially similar to bay heads except that the peat does not accumulate under these trees to the same extent.

Soil. The soil is predominately fine sand in depressions of the Tamiami limestone. Considerable organic matter is present to make a mucky mixture that lies on top of the sand.

Vegetation. The usual species found in the bay heads of the Big Cypress Swamp, Province IX, are found in this association.

Custard Apple Swamps

Around 1900 when farmers moved into the Okeechobee area, they first cleared and utilized the rich, mucky soil underlying the custard apple swamps surrounding the lake.

Custard apple swamp. *This photograph was taken in Pineland Glade No. 2 and is the largest pond apple community found in the Everglades National Park. The trees developed in the perimeter of a large solution hole. Note the great abundance of bromeliads.*

Interior of custard apple swamp. *This interior view of a custard apple swamp was photographed in Monroe County south of the Loop Road.*

These soils were highly productive but lasted only a few years. Fire used in clearing and oxidation from exposure soon destroyed them.

Patches of several hundred acres of these swamps formerly occurred in the Big Cypress swamps of Collier and Monroe counties, in the sloughs of the Tree Island Everglades, and to the east of these sloughs. Only small patches now exist. The largest swamp seen by the writer was of some 50 acres several miles south of the Loop Road in Monroe County. It was damaged in the 1965 fires. Every effort should be made to save this specimen before it is completely destroyed.

Vegetation. Custard or pond apple makes up 50 percent or more of the arborescent stand. The fluted trunks are often over 3 feet in diameter; the crowns intermesh and support numerous epiphytes, Spanish moss, bromeliads, orchids, and ferns. All of the typical swamp hardwoods add sparingly to the species mixture of these stands. Between the buttressed bases, a mesh of waterways exists, through which one can explore by canoe or by wading. The cool, delightful shade of these swamps and the reflected images of the overhanging epiphytes tend to entice one deeper and deeper into the interior.

Saw Grass Marshes

Saw grass marshes once occupied the greatest expanse of all of the associations of the freshwater environments (Provinces IV, VI, VII, VIII, and IX). Even the glades of the pineland were primarily a saw grass sod. Fossils of this association exist beneath the Florida Bay keys, and living

Circular plant communities. *Many of the plant communities of the area develop from a small beginning in a relatively open swamp. They start from a few plants, a wind-borne willow, reed, or cattail seed; a floating red or white mangrove seedling; or a floating seed of saw grass, red or sweet bay, or coco plum that lodges on a slight marl elevation during low water. Once established and uninhibited, they spread outward rapidly until they meet a barrier of another species or until the firm debris base they help establish becomes invaded by other species.*

Saw grass changes to buttonwood. *This photograph taken in a saw grass swamp north of West Lake shows the invasion of saw grass by buttonwood. In this case, the change has been going on for some time, as indicated by the decay-resistant, fire-killed buttonwood trees. Swamp hardwoods and red mangrove are also represented. Saw grass is a remarkable plant. No doubt it formed the great peat beds of the River of Grass, formerly 6 to 8 feet deep in places. Much of this community in the freshwater swamps is rapidly disappearing. Tall, dense saw grass occurs in deep, peaty soil and requires a water coverage of the rhizomes for most of the year. It also formed extensive but shorter and less dense stands on the marl deposit in the freshwater glades, such as those now farmed east of the Pineland Ridge and in the sloughs crossing the pineland. Here much of the peat oxidized each dry season and never formed deep beds. This layer of peat has now practically disappeared, lowering the former land level 6 to 12 inches.*

remnants still exist in the Saline Mangrove Zone, but here they have almost completely been replaced by black rush *(Juncus roemerianus)* or red mangroves. Saw grass grows much taller in the basins of the bedrock, sloughs, and solution holes where water remains longer or throughout the dry periods.

Formerly, when water levels were higher and dry periods shorter, saw grass marshes must have occupied practically all of the freshwater land surface now occupied by freshwater mangroves except for the tree islands and areas of shallow soil. Many great fires have been recorded (Davis, 1943, 1946; Robertson, 1954). Early botanists frequently commented on fires in the 1920s (Small, 1929). Around 1937, after the Labor Day hurricane of 1935 left quantities of debris in the tree islands, much of the Freshwater Swamps province burned. Again, in 1945 to 1947, in 1951 and 1952, and in 1962 and 1965 fires destroyed tremendous expanses of saw grass. The top layers of peat containing the mat of rhizomes were burned to ashes. In some places the peat burned to bedrock or to marl soil. Much roughly eroded limestone formerly covered with peat was exposed in these great fires of the past fifty years. The removal of the deeper peat beds left many ponds scattered over the surface. These are now filled with aquatic plants in the rainy season.

Soils. Saw grass marshes are best developed on the deeper soils, 2 feet or more of built-up peat or marl. The peat is sometimes stratified with layers of gray to darkly stained marl up to several inches in thickness. A layer of dark, tough marl usually lies in the limestone bedrock. Three freshwater shells, Helisoma, Pomacea, and Physa, are common in this marl but not in the saw grass peat.

The glades east of the Pineland Ridge to the mangroves along the shore of Biscayne Bay were formerly extensive saw grass marshes broken by tree islands, chiefly bay heads. This expanse of saw grass was growing on 6 to 12 inches of peat underlaid by 2 to 4 feet of marl containing the freshwater shells Helisoma and Pomacea.

Enormous quantities of peat are formed under saw grass plants. The entire plant dies after inflorescence (flowering), adding its dry bulk to this accumulating organic layer. The deeper layers of this decomposed plant material combined with marl has the property of solidifying into a hard, coal-like mass on drying. The saw grass marsh soils usually have a fairly firm crust of 6 to 8 inches, sufficiently strong to sustain a person's weight. The crust is made up of matted rhizomes.

The scattered distribution of this community is attributed to the recent fires burning into the dry peat, thus destroying the saw grass rhizomes. Seedlings germinating on the new surface die during the next dry season. These fire scars are numerous and distinctive of the saw grass swamps.

Vegetation. The tall, more vigorous saw grass marshes with plants 6 to 10 feet tall are usually of such density that few other plants can survive. Where the soil is shallow, or when the period of water submergence is short, many marsh plants invade the stand. The more abundant and widespread of these are spike rush, beak rushes, arrowhead, maiden cane, spider lily, pickerelweed, and cattails.

No trees are characteristic of these swamps except on the banks of the gator holes. The extensive saw grass swamps support few alligators and, in fact, very few vertebrate animals.

Although the saw grass community is one of those most resistant to change, once broken by farming or altered by deep-burning fires, it can be destroyed. Within a period of ten to twenty years the entire characteristics of the community may change. During the early farming days the saw grass glades were fired, plowed, farmed, and later abandoned; thousands of acres are now covered with swamp hardwoods that a few years ago were saw grass glades on peat soil. These are now replaced by pure willow stands or mixtures of all the swamp hardwood species. In some of these old fields abandoned twenty-five years ago, the line of demarkation between saw grass and swamp hardwoods is still sharp and distinct. Even the saw grass strips between fields that were used for access are still unchanged. In the glade land between the small freshwater creeks where alligators used to be abundant, the old nesting sites of these reptiles served as points of initial entry of the swamp hardwoods on areas that escaped fire for ten or twenty years.

Observations in the 1950s indicated that many burned-over saw grass areas were not reproducing second stands. Study plots were established, and close scrutiny showed that although seedlings were established in great numbers nearly every year on the exposed marl and peat soils, during the years 1962 and 1965 these seedlings all died during the prolonged winter dry period. On July 26, 1966, forty-eight potted plants 12 inches tall were set out on these plots. These failed when the water disappeared in 1967. Another lot of similar plants were set out April 17, 1969. These grew rapidly through that summer. Seeds germinated and grown in potted soil of varying mixtures of peat, periphyton mats, and pure marl all developed well as long as the surface was wet. Those in pots filled with periphyton mats exceeded all others in growth.

The flower stalk of saw grass begins to elongate in March and develops rapidly, flowering in July and producing matured fruit in August. During the 1962 and 1965 periods of rainfall shortage, the flower stalks were one-third to one-half normal height and the seeds were infertile. Saw grass stands submerged by Hurricane Betsy in September 1965 failed to produce flower stalks the following year but did produce fertile seeds in 1967. Plants sprouting after fires rarely produce flower stalks until the second year.

Spike Rush Marshes

This community is characterized by shallow marl soil with a thin surface of periphyton peat. The water disappears early in the dry season and the plants are scattered. The transition from pure stands of saw grass to the spike rush marshes or "Wet Prairies" (Loveless, 1959) is often abrupt, the result of fires destroying the rhizomes of saw grass and the burning off of the surface layer of peat.

These fire-induced communities have increased tremendously in the past thirty years. Here a great variety of glade plants are found. Some of these species occur in large patches of pure stands where pond water remains longer. Here, too, the periphyton stimulated by sunlight is abundant in contrast to its scarcity in the dense saw grass.

Soil. The soil of these marshes, which are also called sedge flats, is a thin marl from 2 or 3 inches to 3.5 feet. Currently it is being precipitated by periphyton activity. This gray, calcareous mud remains after former fires removed the organic material.

These associations are flooded during the hydroperiod, but the surface dries during our ever-lengthening dry periods. The depth and duration of the water is apparently the most important factor in species distribution and local abundance.

Spike rush association. *Spike rush* (Eleocharis cellulosa) *now occupies more marsh area in Province IV than saw grass, It is encouraged by fire, while saw grass is destroyed by long winter dry periods and by fires. Spike rush is typically a plant of the marl beds, where it can compete with the thinner stands of saw grass. In small peaty pockets, however, it grows twice the size of those plants growing on marl. The seeds of this species, one of the few that do not float, sink to the bottom into the soft mud. Dense stands of seedlings appear after fires that burn off the plant stems. In this area red mangrove seedlings invaded in 1965 when it was flooded by Hurricane Betsy. Ninety percent of these have since died during dry periods. The white stake in the photograph is a water level gauge.*

Vegetation. The more abundant herbaceous plants are spike rush *(Eleocharis cellulosa),* beak rush *(Rhynchospora tracyi),* bulrushes, fringe rushes, bladderworts, spider lilies, water dropwort, gerardia, maiden cane, and panic grasses. The seeds of some of these rushes germinate after fires from seed stored in the marl soil.

Ponds

Freshwater ponds are numerous and appear to originate either as depressions in the bedrock, as open patches in the original impoundment behind the Buttonwood Embankment, or as burned-out patches of peat. The latter in former saw grass swamps often cover several acres. These freshwater ponds are commonly inhabited by spatterdocks, water lilies, and other submerged aquatic plants. The numerous smaller ponds were once kept open by alligators, but many of these have closed since 1962. Brackish water types of ponds are described under Province III.

Creek Banks

The banks of the creeks that penetrate into the Freshwater Swamps from the mangrove estuaries are slightly elevated above the land level of the interior. The vegetation of these raised banks gradually loses more and more of the salt-tolerant species inland.

Buttonwood becomes the dominant tree, and red mangrove is pushed to the water's edge or, with white mangrove, into the interior freshwater swamps. The narrow fringe of red mangrove that overhangs the water is noticeable as a white line on the aerial photograph of the Roberts River. If the creek water is deeper than about 2 feet, the prop roots do not become rooted and leafy branches overhang. Where the mud is shallower, prop roots push out into the creek, a useful guide when running a skiff in these shallow waters.

Soil. Red mangrove peat is exposed at the water's edge and extends inland under hammock peat. Beneath both of these sediments lies a marl base varying in thickness to bedrock; this is often stratified with saw grass or mangrove peat, varying as the banks meander. Older creeks may show a profile of hammock peat almost to bedrock.

Vegetation. Hammock peat builds up under the buttonwoods occupying higher ground, and other hardwoods become established—wax myrtle, randia, poisonwood, myrsine, red bay, pond apple, dove plum, and palmettos. As the creeks push into the saw grass, the banks are less elevated, the arborescent vegetation disappears, and the tiny creeks become alligator trails ending in ponds.

Casuarina and Other Exotics

Egler (1932) described with some concern the rapid and complete invasion of casuarina, or Australian pine, over the marl soils of Dade County. He stated that this tree was in an "active process of establishing itself in its own vegetational equilibrium." Egler pointed out that this light-demanding tree that produces winged seeds distributed by wind is rapidly invading many sites to the exclusion of native plants. Although fires, frosts, and hurricanes, together with a shift in agricultural practices, have destroyed a considerable percentage of the stands that Egler saw in 1932 during his study of the "Southeast Saline Everglades," this plant is still advancing on the exposed marl soils of the higher and drying glades, on the sand and shell beaches of the Gulf coast, and on the Florida Bay keys.

Casuarina does best on mineral soil without competing vegetation. It advances most rapidly on recently abandoned farm land and on beaches disturbed by hurricanes. It does not seem to become established in any of the mangrove associations or in glade lands that are flooded most of the

Australian pines. *These pines invaded Highland Beach with Hurricane Donna in 1960, when seeds and even large branches bearing cones were deposited. A year later this beach, over 100 feet wide, was colonized with scattered seedlings 12 to 18 inches tall. These grew rapidly and produced seeds three years later that have developed into a solid stand. All indigenous vegetation was crowded out, and dead and dying plants of many native species can be seen in the understory.*

Melaleuca. *This photograph shows a former cypress head that has been invaded by melaleuca. One cypress, still alive, can be seen in the left background. This tree, commonly called cajeput, is also invading the saw grass swamp of conservation areas north of the Tamiami Trail in Dade and Broward counties. Unless destroyed, they will in time occupy extensive areas of these swamps, destroying their recreational values.*

year. East of US 1 from Homestead to Canal C-111, many of the bay heads have been invaded by casuarina and the native species of swamp hardwoods are being shaded out. It presents a most serious problem in the preservation of native vegetation in South Florida.

Three other exotics are invading the plant associations of the area: Brazilian holly *(Shinus terebinthfolius),* cajeput *(Melaleuca quirquenervia),* and ardisia *(Ardisia solanacea).* The indiscriminate introduction of exotic plants needs federal regulation. None should be propagated and distributed until their propensity to reproduce naturally and invade our native environment is determined. Those already here present a formidable problem in the management of the Everglades National Park. The cost of control in the next few years will run into hundreds of thousands of dollars, and at that it is questionable if satisfactory suppression can be obtained.

PROVINCE V – PINELAND RIDGE

Also called the Rockland Ridge, this area is an outcrop of Miami oolite that forms an eastern coastal ridge impounding the Everglades for some fifty miles. The maximum elevation of 20 feet in the vicinity of Miami gradually lowers to 8 to 9 feet as the ridge extends southwest through Homestead and on some twenty miles to Mahogany Hammock in Everglades National Park, where it is 1.5 to 2.0 feet above mean sea level. This rock land has an extremely rough, pitted, irregular surface, much of it so eroded that it is called pinnacle rock, a formation that is difficult to cross by walking. It is perforated with numerous solution holes, basins, and caves and is crossed by several sloughs that before the drainage period carried an overflow of water from the Everglades swamp to the coast.

Geology

A thick, porous block of limestone composed of two facies underlie this province; the upper is an oolitic limestone of Pleistocene age and is broken by many solution holes, caves, and fissures. The lower is a Bryozoan limestone of the Sangamon period (Hoffmeister, et al., 1967). Together they form the Miami limestone. The upper formation is extensively used for winter agriculture or is being rapidly developed for town sites.

Soil and Hydrology

This high, porous, oolitic limestone is watered by rainfall and is well drained. The water table is now lowered from 3 to 6 feet in the Homestead area. Even the glades are dry except after heavy rains. The soil under the hardwood hammocks and in the solution holes consists chiefly of decomposed limestone mixed with organic matter. The glade land is composed of 1 to 4 feet of marl, the upper portion well mixed with organic materials. Nearly all the capping of surface peat is now gone. In the Miami area, sand often fills the solution holes and covers the rock surface. Here the soil is more acid, supporting heaths. In the Redlands area, a dense red soil covers the limestone and fills the solution holes. Small patches of this red soil are found on the surface of the gray limestone after fires. It is brought up by termites to fill their feeding galleries constructed in stumps and dead logs. When fires consume these termite-infested logs, a cast of the red soil is left on the surface among the ashes (Craighead, 1970).

The limestone itself has little fertility, but the organic matter in the numerous cavities provides nutrients for the varied flora. When cleared for agriculture, 3 to 4 inches of the surface rock is broken with heavy machinery. The humus is mixed with the limestone thereby, and liberal quantities of fertilizer are added, after which good crops may be grown for two years. The fields are then left fallow for two to five years. Lately, experimental work of the Agricultural Extension Service indicates the value of cover crops to replace organic matter.

Vegetation

Formerly a continuous stand of Dade County pine spotted with tropical hardwood hammocks formed the arborescent flora. Shrubby and herbaceous species formed an understory of tropical hardwoods, and nearly 100 shrubby or herbaceous endemics are kept under control by periodic fires. The glades and larger solution holes support typically swamp plants, grasses, sedges, and swamp hardwoods.

Plant Associations

Except for the pineland itself, most of the plant communities are represented by small patches or keys within this province. Five of the most important communities, namely Pinelands, Tropical Hardwood Hammocks, Pineland Sloughs, Scrub Buttonwood, and Glades, are described. The others, Cypress Domes, Willow Heads, Custard Apple Swamps, Spikerush Marshes, and Solution Holes, are described under Province IV, Freshwater Swamps.

Pinelands

Dade County pine formerly covered all of the limestone

ridge extending from North Miami along both sides of US 1 and on in a southwesterly, curving direction to Mahogany Hammock. Its total length is about 55 miles; it is some 4 to 5 miles wide at several places of its greatest breadth. Numerous rock outcrops on the north side of this ridge and in Province VI (Low Pinelands and Sloughs) were also forested with pine. Township 56S R37E, formerly in Everglades National Park, had a good stand of pine that was completely destroyed by fires in 1951 and 1952. Along the margins of the ridge, particularly the one facing Province IV, Freshwater Swamps, a narrow fringe of pine grows on thin marl soil.

The early homes in Dade County were built of Dade County pine. It is so dense, so resistant to decay, and so hard that when dry a special steel nail must be used or holes must be bored to receive nails. The heartwood is resistant to termite attack, and many of the homes of fifty years or more of age are still in good condition today. During World War II "everything that would make a two-by-four" was cut except for a few isolated patches in the Park. The owner of a local saw mill operating in 1952 told me that in the virgin stands of Dade County pine many trees were 2 feet in diameter and as much as 90 feet tall.

Soil. In the Miami area, the solution holes in the rock land are filled with sand and the soil is acid. This portion was named as a distinct association by Harper (1927). In the southern two-thirds of the ridge, the depressions are filled with marl or peat and the soil is alkaline except for some of the peat in the deeper solution holes. The marginal pine growing on marl soil and formerly flooded much of the year has been called "Low Pineland." The pineland association outside of the Park is rapidly disappearing to agriculture and development. Most of the hammocks have been destroyed, although a few exceptional ones have been bought by Dade County for perservation, notably Matheson, Simpson, Brickell, Owaissa Bauer, Costellow, and Fuchs hammocks. Several pieces of pineland of less than 100 acres are also in these parks.

Vegetation. Most of the plants of Dade County can be found in the pineland if one includes the microenviron-

Pineland with slash pine. *Slash pine, locally called Dade County pine, occupied practically all of the higher rock land of the three-county area except the upper Florida Keys. This higher rock land was rapidly cleared after 1900 for lumber, homesites, and later for farming. Now there is little mature pine left in Dade County except in the Everglades National Park. Pine, a light-demanding tree, is crowded out by the intrusion of hardwoods. Pure stands are perpetuated by light fires. Stands in the Park are managed by the use of controlled fires every three to four years. An interesting feature of the pinelands is the number of endemic plants, about 100, that are all adapted to a fire regime. The pineland is rapidly disappearing as land is cleared for farms and residential development. Generally speaking, reproduction in the existing stands of Dade County pine are poor. The frequent fires no doubt play a part in this situation by destroying the very small seedlings in their first year after germination. Good seed years are not too frequent. Winter and spring fires before the September seedfall remove much competing vegetation and excess duff, and permit the seeds to germinate on mineral soil. Seedlings do not survive well on a thick layer of duff. Seedling survival appears to coincide with 2 or 3 fireless seasons after germination and well distributed precipitation through the normally dry winter season.*

ments of the glades, swamps, hammocks, and solution holes. Even red mangrove and the coastal halophytes intermingle with pine along the coast of Collier County. The more common trees in the pine stands are Dade County pine, rough leaf, bustic, varnish leaf, blolly, pineland olive, shortleaf fig, byrsonima, tetrazygia, myrsine, saw palmetto, poisonwood, marlberry, sumac, satinleaf, shinus, and silver palm. Two ferns are common, ladder brake and anemia.

Many shrubs and herbaceous plants are found, a large number of which are endemic.

A most interesting plant of the pineland is a grass locally called fire grass *(Andropogon cabanisii)*. This abundant grass develops as numerous gray-green tufts in the tiny pits and crevices of the gray limestone. It remains in the vegetative stage until a fire flashes over the clumps. Soon they begin to develop flower stalks, which reach 5 to 8 feet in height, forming a dense understory that when mature suggests a wheat field ready for harvest.

Another plant of the pineland once extensively utilized is the coontie *(Zamia integrifolia)*. This small cycad has a large tuberous root of several pounds in weight that is high in starch content. It formed a staple portion of the diet of the early Indians, the Seminoles, and the early white men. The starch must be thoroughly leached to remove poisonous alkaloids.

Tropical Hardwood Hammocks

The term tropical hardwood hammock is applied to the tree islands that occur on the higher rock land, in the pinelands, and on rock mesas in the glades that rise 1 to 3 feet above the adjacent glade surface. These are formed on remnants of the former higher rock land that escaped degradation. Small (1930a) referred to them as "Everglade Keys." While it may seem difficult to become accustomed to the wide local use of the term "key" in this kind of context, it does not take too much of a stretch of the imagination to move from a sandy key surrounded by water to a forested Florida Bay key to a forested "island" on the mainland surrounded by pine. Similar communities occur on the scattered rock outcrops in Collier and western Monroe counties.

Probably over 500 tropical hardwood hammocks formerly dotted the pineland of Dade County. They ranged in size from one-fourth acre to over 100 acres. Some 125 hammocks occur on Long Pine Key in the Park. These were well known and were named and roughly mapped by the tree snail collectors of forty to fifty years ago.

These hammocks stimulated many colorful descriptions

Tropical hardwood hammocks. *The hammocks dotting the pineland were the prized attraction in our local flora for early botanical explorers. They were described many times, and several theories for their existence were advanced. Epiphytic orchids and bromeliads were abundant, encouraged by a moist, equitable microclimate that was cooler in summer and warmer in winter than surrounding temperatures. Few hammocks have remained unscathed. Four mahogany hammocks in the Park and part of Paradise Key are partially intact.*

The larger trees, 4 to 6 feet in diameter, are over 200 years of age. A few fine hammocks between Homestead and Miami preserved as city or county parks are becoming damaged by recreational activities. Beginning around 1910, tree snails in these hammocks became popular collectors' items. Keen rivalry developed to corner new varieties. All of the area was thoroughly combed, and the hammocks were all named, often after prominent biologists. A list of these hammock names is a miniature "Who's Who." Later, when epiphytic orchids came into demand, they were collected with equal enthusiasm. They are still being sought, and in the writer's experience at least three species appear to have been exterminated in the past ten years.

Strangler fig. *A common inhabitant of the hammocks, this interesting plant begins life as an epiphyte high in a host tree where sunlight is available. The seeds are carried by birds, which relish the fruit. Later, long aerial roots extend to the ground and rapidly form a trunk with many side branches. These often envelop the host and finally kill it.*

of this country by early botanists. Most of the hammocks have been destroyed in the last thirty to fifty years. Some good examples, however, are Mahogany Hammock and the south end of Paradise Key in the Park, and Owaissa Bauer and Costellow hammocks just north of Homestead, as well as the several in Miami previously mentioned.

The genesis of hammock formation was a favorite topic of discussion by many early naturalists in Florida. Simpson's 1920 proposal in his fascinating descriptions of early Florida's natural history seem to be as satisfactory as any. He calls attention to the greater abundance of solution holes in the hammocks as compared to the adjacent pineland. These, he pointed out, often carry water (or so they did twenty years ago) throughout the year and serve to maintain a humid atmosphere necessary for the accumulation of peat, the luxuriant ground cover of ferns, and the abundant epiphytes. Again, there may actually be a local difference in the physical and chemical composition of the limestone in these places, as is maintained by local farmers who consistently avoid clearing certain of these lands for cultivation.

Soil. The rock elevations on which these hammocks occur are usually about 1.0 to 1.5 feet above the surrounding pineland and as much as 3 to 4 feet above the surface in the glades. On top of this rock is a layer of hammock peat 6 inches or more in thickness (depending on recent fire history). The rock surface as seen after fires is extremely dissected, and actually there is very little soil left except in the solution holes. These are filled with peat or marl depending on the severity and frequency of past fires. The few remains of organic soil are a woody peat, hammock or Gandy peat, similar to that described under bay heads in Province IV, Freshwater Marshes. Marl may occupy the deeper portions of the burned-out solution holes.

In the larger hammocks that have escaped fires over many years, a loamy soil cover builds up on the rock surface to a depth of 0.5 to 1.5 feet. This may also fill the solution holes. Such soils were the foundation for the luxurious growth of the tropical hardwoods present when white man first arrived. Stumps and logs still present on the virgin hammock floors are much larger than any of the present living trees.

Vegetation. Except for a few shrubs and trees migrating from the north, the flora of these hammocks is composed primarily of tropical hardwood species. The more characteristic trees in the hammocks of the Pineland Ridge, like those of the Freshwater Swamps, include live oak, gumbo-limbo, lysiloma, bustic, pond apple (in solution holes), dove plum, white and Simpson's stoppers, poisonwood, myrsine, marlberry, mahogany, wild lime, and hog plum. Vines include wild bamboo, possum grape, hippocratea, Virginia creeper, poison ivy, devil's claw, morinda, and chicken grape. Bromeliads and orchids are abundant and give a tropical atmosphere to the shady interiors (Craighead, 1963).

When fires destroy these hammocks in the pineland or on the rock mesas of the glades, some roots usually survive. The regeneration from root suckers produces a new stand that is practically identical to the old. Repeated fires, however, destroy all of the hardwoods in time.

Many hammocks have a dense bank of saw palmettos forming their perimeters. This bank may be 20 to 100 feet wide. It serves as an excellent firebreak, shelter for rattlesnakes, and can cause much trouble for the hiker unless he can find a deer trail to follow into the interior.

Pineland Sloughs

This vegetation type sharply contrasts with the pinelands. Thirteen sloughs cross or nearly cross the rock land. The widest (1.5 miles) is Taylor Slough in Everglades National Park. These sloughs formerly supported saw grass, willow heads, pond apple heads, and grasses. Considerable numbers were cultivated by the early farmers but are now the sites of the numerous drainage canals. They may even be utilized for developments if the canals can keep them drained, but it is more likely that the heavy precipitation from hurricanes will always present flooding problems on the marl soil.

Vegetation. Dense, luxuriant saw grass formerly occupied a considerable area of these sloughs with their several inches to a foot of marl soil. Besides saw grass, other sedges, several grasses, and higher plants such as oxypolis and aeschynom-

Pineland slough. *A portion of Taylor Slough just south of Park Headquarters is illustrated here. The swamp hardwoods shown came in on farmland cultivated for several years before 1947 when the Park was established. In no case in the writer's experience has broken saw grass sod returned to its original plant cover. A few pine trees to the rear mark the margin of this pineland slough. The crushed saw grass trail was made by man with fire equipment in 1968. Such trails made prior to 1947 are still clearly discernible by the change in vegetation from saw grass to spike rush, where the compacted soil is deeper. On the slightly raised margins of the ruts, swamp hardwoods become established. Many such trails criss-cross the glades of the Park, and more and more are added each year. In the Big Cypress, extensive areas of the original vegetation have been destroyed by glades buggies and airboat trails.*

ene were common, and most of the species mentioned under spike rush marshes in Province IV were once present. Virgin vegetation can be seen in certain places in the Park, but fires and the lowered water table have removed most of these stands. With the completion of the canals across the Pineland Ridge, these sloughs are now dry most of the year. Formerly they provided important feeding grounds for wading birds, but since 1962 they have practically been abandoned.

Scrub Buttonwood

Between the pinelands and the glades, in the highly dissected and rough limestone, stands of nearly pure buttonwood are frequent. Here the trees are short, from 6 to 15 feet high, bear numerous branches, and form in clumps. This is the result of occasional frosts and to some extent fires, although fires are seldom excessively hot in these stands because of the lack of ground cover. Under normal moisture conditions this community offers a good fire brake, but when very dry the organic accumulations in the rock pits are consumed and many trees killed. The soil is thin or lacking on the rough, exposed, rocky surface, but the numerous solution holes are often well-filled with peat and leaf accumulations.

Vegetation. As this community merges into the glades or the low pineland, other swamp hardwoods are present. Scattered pines may be found on the higher rocks. The rough bark of the buttonwood encourages bromeliads and epiphytic orchids, often presenting excellent displays of these plants.

Roadbed scar. *The early road to Paradise Key made in 1915 was replaced in 1947. Although all the fill was removed to glade level, the vegetation is completely altered by the compaction of the soil. This well illustrates the delicate balance between many of the various plant associations.*

Glades

The term glades as used by the early farmers implied a treeless, level, prairie-like association. The vegetation was chiefly saw grass, together with a few other grasses and sedges on peaty or marly soils of variable depth. In addition to the large transverse sloughs many small glades spot the Pineland Ridge. The soil usually consists of 6 to 18 inches of marl.

Vegetation. Few other plants occur in the better strands of saw grass. On thinner soils a number of marsh plants occur, such as marsh pink, lobelia, loosestrife, oxypolis, aeschynomene, asclepias, lippia, capraria, mecardonia, utricularia, justicia, and tall goldenrod.

PROVINCE VI – LOW PINELAND AND SLOUGHS

This province is characterized by its rough, rocky outcropping of limestone eroded into pinnacle rock at many places. It ranges from 1.5 to 5.0 feet in elevation and is poorly drained. Many small, rough limestone mesas of one-tenth acre to 25 acres spot the area. The eastern margin slopes off the Pineland Ridge, and the western margin forms a low boundary usually not passable by airboats from the Shark River Slough.

Geology, Soil, and Hydrology

The surface rock of Province VI is composed of Miami oolitic limestone of the Pleistocene age with some of the underlying Bryozoan limestones outcropping. Hammock peat lies beneath hardwoods and bay heads; thin marl deposits are present in the sloughs, with some saw grass peat. Hammock and pineland are slightly above water most of the year. All other sites are subject to flooding from the Shark River Slough during heavy rains. The lower center of this province forms the watershed for Taylor Slough. Practically all of this province lies east of the Park.

Vegetation

Tropical hardwood hammocks are frequent throughout the area, as well as many patches of pine; both are found on the rock outcrops. Bay heads and swamp plants exist in the sloughs and on the lower ground. There is considerable palmetto on the marl soils of the eastern portions. These once-flooded areas are rapidly being cleared for cultivation or construction.

Plant Associations

Practically all of the principal plant associations typical of the freshwater areas are found here. Except for some of the hammocks, which are the largest in the Park, the associations are broken into small fragments. For the most part, previous descriptions for Provinces IV and V are applicable here.

Tropical Hardwood Hammocks

A number of large hammocks characterize this area; they are found on low rock mesas about 1 to 2.5 feet above the surrounding levels. They usually have a firm surface of Gandy peat greatly thinned by fire. Live oak is a predominant species. Some of the tropical hardwoods of the coastal hammocks are wanting, while a few others such as black ironwood are found far inland.

Pine Islands

The Dade County pine in this province is found scattered on rough rocky outcrops, where it is frequently mixed with tropical hardwoods and palmettos. Many of the better stands have been destroyed by the frequent fires of the past thirty years, to such an extent that only a few stumps are left.

Saw Grass Marshes

This community is also much broken and confined to smaller sloughs except for the extensive and rather thinly stocked stands of saw grass prairie in the northeastern portion of this province. These have recently nearly all been burned, broken, and farmed or developed. As the Everglades peat disappeared, pinnacle rock and marl were exposed and had to be ground up by bulldozers. Some of the crops on both sides of Florida Route 27 south of US 41 have been remarkably free of frost damage.

Spike Rush Swamps, Bay Heads, and Willow Heads

These associations are numerous and are essentially as described under Province IV, Freshwater Swamps.

PROVINCE VII – TREE ISLAND EVERGLADES

The name Tree Island Everglades is used for the southern extension of the great Everglades marsh. The northern portion in Broward and Palm Beach counties, except for the agricultural areas that are rapidly increasing, is still covered by an almost continuous saw grass community. Tree islands begin to appear in the Everglades slough some 45 miles south of Lake Okeechobee, near where Levee 5 crosses Conservation Area 3, and increase in numbers toward the south to where this province meets the freshwater mangroves. This southern portion of the Everglades, characterized by its numerous tree islands, extends in a southwesterly direction for some 25 miles into the Park. The portion within the Park is also often spoken of as the Shark River Slough.

Limestone outcrops are frequent, becoming more so toward the east and west margins. The entire area is spotted with tree islands, which are usually lenticular in shape and molded to the drainage pattern. Remains of saw grass peat indicate that as late as 1900 saw grass communities may have covered much of the area between the tree islands.

Geology

The bedrock is chiefly Bryozoan limestone (Hoffmeister et al., 1967). There are numerous outcrops along the rock reefs and at the heads of the tree islands, and the limestone outcrops along the east and west margins of the slough prevent the use of airboats. The overburden of peat and marl is of Recent origin and is alkaline except under the deeper saw grass peat.

Soil and Hydrology

The southern end at the present time has a much shallower soil than the true saw grass Everglades to the north.

Primarily marl, much of it at present is only 12 to 18 inches deep. At the extreme southern end between the small creeks the soils may reach 4 to 6 feet in depth. Peat beds of small size under willow heads, pickerelweed, and saw grass sloughs often reach 4 to 5 feet in depth.

Several varieties of peat and marl have been described. Much of the deep saw grass peat has been destroyed in the past forty years, leaving roughly eroded limestone exposed. Much of this burned area is temporarily replaced by willow and other swamp hardwoods. Gandy peat lies under the hammocks and bay heads. Practically none of the soil is cultivated. Nearly all of this area outside the Park is within conservation areas and is completely flooded during the rainy season.

Formerly the part of the slough within the Park was covered with water for much of the year. This came from rainfall and from the conservation areas to the north of the Tamiami Trail. From 1962 to 1965 the dry period was greatly extended, and ample water was received only after the gates were opened from Conservation Area 3 late in 1965. Surplus water moves very slowly through the vegetation and rapidly disappears by evaporation and transpiration. This loss is estimated to equal the average annual rainfall (Johnson, 1958).

Historically, this vast Everglades slough, often called the "River of Grass," extended from Lake Okeechobee to the tributaries of the Shark River. The Everglades forms one of the largest freshwater swamps on the North American continent. It formerly occupied nearly one-third of the area of southern Florida. When white men first attempted to invade it, it was roughly 100 miles long by 40 miles wide. At that time, summer rainfall and, rarely, some overflow from Lake Okeechobee filled this vast swamp with several feet of water. Overflow from Lake Okeechobee has been insignificant in this century (Johnson, 1958).

At times during the dry season, however, the Everglades slough was without surface water except for the deeper ponds and sloughs, many of which reached bedrock 3 to 10 feet below. Drainage, which began about 1900, has greatly altered the character of this swamp. The lower water levels

Tree Island Everglades. *Also known as the Shark River Slough, this province normally carries water except during the dry winters and spring. Much of its water supply came from rainfall; the remainder comes from the flow north of the Tamiami Trail, now conservation areas. It is spotted with many long lens-shaped tree islands whose axes conform to the drainage pattern. A rock outcrop is often present on the upstream end of these islands, while the long central axes follow a depression in the bedrock. The high land is rarely completely flooded, and supports tropical hardwood forests. The lower land is occupied by swamp hardwoods, margined and tailed with rank saw grass. As the margins of the Shark River Slough rise slightly to the east and west, the tree islands take on the usual circular form that characterizes most of the plant communities when they are not competing with other restricting forces.*

Accompanying the recent drainage in dry years, fires burned in long tongues, following the drier peat. Here rhizomes of the saw grass were killed. New plants revegetate slowly, and a sharp line of demarkation remains for many years (foreground). Thus, much peat is removed that once formed a great water storage reservoir for this ecosystem. Now bare marl and rock form the bottom of these dry swamps in winter. During the rainy season ponds form in these depressions. They are now largely filled with water lilies and other submerged aquatics. In other words, these peaty reservoirs are now lakes subject to rapid loss of water by evaporation.

permitted the drying of the surface peat during the ever-lengthening winter and spring waterless periods. The accompanying fires removed much peat, especially in the southern portion where the bedrock was nearer the surface, leaving the peat thinner and subject to greater dessication. This has resulted in profound and extensive changes in the Park, where massive saw grass beds and many tree islands have been destroyed. For more complete descriptions of earlier conditions see Harshberger (1914), Small (1933), Harper (1927), and Loveless (1959).

The recent (1967-1970) flooding of Conservation Area 3 has greatly altered the vegetation, destroying most of the tree islands on the eastern side and practically changing the area into a shallow lake.

Vegetation

Most of the plant communities except for those of the Saline Mangrove Zone are represented in the Tree Island Everglades. Saw grass and spike rush marshes are numerous, and large tree islands occur. The rock outcrops are covered with hammock growth, and some have considerable palmetto. Bay heads with swamp hardwoods are numerous, and some cypress on peat deposits are found in the extreme southern portion. The other associations represent emergent vegetation; their bases are covered with water during the rainy season. Ponds are also large and numerous.

Plant Associations

Six principal plant associations of the Tree Island Everglades are described; these are Tropical Hardwood Hammocks, Saw Grass Marshes, Bay Heads, Willow Heads, Spike Rush Marshes, and Ponds.

Tropical Hardwood Hammocks

The tree islands in this province occur on small rock mesas 1 to 3 feet above the glade level. These occur either as isolated islands along the narrow rock reefs that criss-cross the Park or on the upstream tips of the long, lenticular bay heads that have formed behind them. They are essentially similar to the pineland hammocks of Province IV, Freshwater Swamps, except that several tropical hardwoods found near the coast and on the Florida Keys are lacking, and several northern hardwoods such as hackleberry and water oak are more abundant.

Many tree islands show the effects of early Indian use in the abundant pottery shards of the Calusas and the citrus and bananas introduced by the Seminoles. Fishpoison vines are frequent. Hackberry, persimmon, mulberry, potato tree, and palmetto are likewise common, sometimes in pure stands, and were probably planted for their fruits.

Saw Grass Marshes

The saw grass marshes, or swamps, of the Tree Island Everglades are essentially similar to the saw grass marshes described for the Freshwater Swamps. The better examples that have not been burned out completely are at the northern end of the Shark River Slough, outside the Park near the Tamiami Trail, and between the freshwater creeks of the

Tree island in Shark River Slough. *This tree island shows the tropical hardwood hammock on the upstream end, where it grows on a rock outcrop. The remainder is composed of swamp hardwoods on peat beds 2 to 4 feet deep. This portion of the island lies in a depression of the bedrock. This fissure dates back several thousands of years and is no doubt being slowly etched deeper. In the distance (to the east) appears the higher land of Province VI spotted with many circular tree islands.*

Flooding of tree islands. *This tree island in the Shark River Slough shows the effects of the continued recent flooding of the past 3 years. Many trees are dying, chiefly holly, red bay, and wax myrtle. Nature designed these communities for a climate of wet summers and dry winters. Too much water is just as destructive as too little, probably more so.*

Saw grass in Shark River Slough. *In the lower portions of the Shark River Slough, the saw grass and peat have not been so completely destroyed. Water is retained longer in this area, and here the peat is 4 feet deep. The dark community in the foreground is a pickerelweed slough on a deep soil of muck. The tree island to the rear is a rocky outcrop carrying tropical hardwoods and considerable hackberry.*

tributaries. At both places the soil is 4 to 6 feet deep, with peat forming the upper stratum and darkly stained marl beneath on bedrock.

Bay Heads

Bay heads are probably the most characteristic feature of this province. Most of these are elongated, sometimes over 1 mile in length. The soil and vegetation are similar to the bay heads described for the Freshwater Swamps, but red mangrove rarely enters into the composition of this province except where the small creeks finger into the saw grass marshes. An island of red mangrove lies about 1 mile northeast of the Pahayokee Tower.

Willow Heads

Willow has increased enormously in this province in the past thirty years. It is no longer confined to bay heads and gator holes, but has taken over much of the marl soil exposed by oxidation of the peat accompanying the receding waters and fires. Thousands of acres are now covered with scrubby willow, not only in this province but on the abandoned agricultural soils southeast of Homestead and Florida City. This has also happened within the Park— around Park headquarters, on Pine Island, and on the extreme western end of the so-called Farm Road. Here saw grass beds were broken up for farming in the early 1930s but were abandoned when the Park took over in 1947. These soils are now covered with dense stands of willow, red bay, dahoon holly, and some cypress. Around the Anhinga Trail some 6 inches of peat has built up under the willows and saw grass since the old Ingraham Highway was constructed about 1915, damming the water to the north.

Many of these willow heads contained clear ponds in their centers, some 8 to 10 feet deep and rarely 20 feet. On careful approach, the bedrock could be seen on the bottom, and numerous fishes, the largest of which were bass, gar, and mudfish, would be quietly drifting back and forth. It has always been a puzzle to explain how the alligator kept these deep ponds clear of vegetation.

Spike Rush Marshes

These are similar to those of the Freshwater Swamps. In most cases they probably represent burned-out saw grass peat that has exposed the underlying marl. They are flooded during the wet season and are usually dry during the winter.

Ponds

Ponds in the Shark River Slough are either large shallow basins floored with marl and flooded in the wet season with 18 to 24 inches of water, or relatively deep (4 to 9 feet) gator holes. The former are the result of fires burning off the peat above the marl base. Formerly they often retained water through the dry season.

Vegetation. Submerged plants make up the majority of this flora: spatterdocks, floating hearts, white and yellow water lilies, bladderworts, water milfoils, mermaid weed, pondweed, and naiads. The margins of the ponds blend into the spike rush swamps and carry the usual emergent sedges, grasses, and flowering plants of that community. The gator holes are normally deep and clear and the ponds devoid of vegetation when occupied by alligators.

PROVINCE VIII – HAMMOCK AND CYPRESS RIDGE

This province lies almost entirely above the Tamiami Trail but does extend south into the Park for some 10 miles in the vicinity of Forty Mile Bend. This is an area of broken rock ridges with intervening depressions occupied by thin marl and sand along the western border. The formations tend in a southwesterly direction to meet the glades along the landward margin of the Freshwater Swamps. This province has the highest land in the Park, about 7 feet above mean sea level. It extends northward through Collier County, forming the western ridge that impounds the Everglades. Here elevations rise to as much as 10 feet.

Geology, Soil, and Hydrology

The bedrock and outcrops of this province are Tamiami limestone of Miocene age. Along the eastern edge it is overlapped by Bryozoan limestone. The soils include hammock peat under the tree islands, mucky peat under the cypress heads, some saw grass peat, and marl in the poorly drained areas that are covered with scrub cypress. This province stands out chiefly because its elevation forms a divide between Provinces VII and IX. It is watered entirely by rainfall. The vegetation is adjusted to the dry winter period. Normally a wet country, during the dry periods of 1962 and 1965 serious fires killed much mature hardwood and cypress as they destroyed the peaty material around their roots. Although higher than the Big Cypress Swamp (Province IX) or the Tree Island Everglades (Province VII), the rather impervious limestone is shallowly eroded into water-retaining basins that hold sufficient water to support bay heads, cypress domes, and extensive scrub cypress stands. The rainfall here exceeds that of most other stations in the three county area, except Miami (Sass, 1967).

Vegetation

The plant associations in this province are in general similar to those described for Province V, Pineland Ridge, and Province IX, Big Cypress Swamp, with a blending of some northern species. Large hammocks, bay heads, cypress domes, and sloughs with much drawf cypress and patches of saw grass and spike rush swamps between occur here.

The limestone elevations were formerly carpeted with some of the finest tropical hardwood hammocks. Many large palmetto hammocks occur in the southern part of this province. Both of these are relatively fire-resistant, and many still persist. The same species of tropical hardwoods are present here as have been previously described, though lacking are some species restricted to the Florida Keys.

Live oak, water oak, lysiloma, gumbo-limbo, two species of eugenia (white stopper and twinberry), and poisonwood are abundant, and bustic is common. Occasionally black ironwood is found. Water oak is common in the bay heads and cypress strands. The vine fern is found abundantly in many hammocks.

Pine forest in Collier County. *Pine and cypress grow side by side on the ponded Tamiami Limestone of Collier County. Pine is established on the higher rock land. This site is also occupied by the tall grass erianthus, indicating frequent flooding. Peat is slow to accumulate here because of repeated light fires. A layer of sand overlies the bedrock.*

Plant Associations

The other principal plant associations—Tropical Hardwood Hammocks, Saw Grass Marshes, Spike Rush Marshes, Ponds, Pine Islands, and Scrub Cypress—have all been described elsewhere.

Pinelands

On the higher rock land along the western portion of this province and to the east in the vicinity of Pinecrest there formerly were some excellent stands of Dade County pine. Most of these were cut for lumber, some without the owners' knowledge. Only a few acres here and there have escaped the saw.

PROVINCE IX – BIG CYPRESS SWAMP

A large, basin-like area including practically all of Collier County except some high land on the east, a coastal sandy strip on the west, all of western Monroe County, and a narrow band of freshwater swamps along the Park boundary are included in this province. The topography presents a series of low limestone outcrops, with numerous sloughs, shallow ponds, and sandy or marl prairies. Several large sloughs transverse the area in a southwesterly direction. One of them, Gum Slough, trends nearly due west to meet the Saline Mangrove Zone (Province III) and partially separates Provinces IV and IX. The elevation ranges from 12 to 40 feet in the north, lowering to mean sea level where the zone meets the freshwater mangroves of Province IV.

Geology

This province is characterized by Tamiami limestone of Miocene age, a rather impervious rock containing much quartz sand that remains in the depressions as the rock breaks down and quartz sand of the Pamlico and Anastasia formations. It is scalloped by many basins and cut by sloughs. It is not dissected into pinnacle rock as is the Miami limestone.

Soil and Hydrology

The soil is often pure sand, marl, or mixtures, 2 to 24 inches deep on the surface of the limestone, and much peat of various kinds fills the depressions of the bedrock. Thin marl or sand is found under the prairies and dwarf cypress. These soils deepen near the mangroves. Some of the fine sands are quite impervious.

The area is watered only by rainfall, averaging around 50 inches. Water is often 12 to 24 inches deep or deeper in the sloughs. The land is poorly drained and, after the initial runoff of heavy rains, has no noticeable water flow. Water levels in the sand and peat were lowered some 1 to 2 feet below normal during 1962 and 1965, but most of the area was under water during the March rainfall of 1969. High waters gradually drain to the south and west to water Province IV and to meet the coastal strip of mangroves or sand dunes. Over much of the area the shallow water forms ponds lasting much of the year.

In the coastal sand dunes is a rather shallow aquifer that

presently supplies the rapidly developing towns. Another source of industrial water is the Florida aquifer some 600 to 700 feet below. This is highly charged with sulphur and must be treated before use for household purposes.

To the north and east of Immokalee and extending into Hendry County lies an area known as Devils Gardens. This is a low swampy land filled with ponds of nearly circular outline. The writer has flown over this area several times and has visited it often. It is a most intriguing community and needs further study to explain the formation of the round ponds rimmed by shrubby and arborescent vegetation.

Vegetation

The vegetation of this province is characterized by cypress strands or sloughs 4 to 6 feet deep, many of which formerly carried trees of high commercial value. Pine or tropical hardwood hammocks appear on the rocky outcrops. Bay heads, pond apple swamps, and pop ash domes are located in the depressions. The rock outcrops often form abrupt islands. Huckleberry, an acid-loving plant, grows in the understory of the pinelands. Red maple and paurotis palms are frequent in the bay heads and cypress strands. Drought and fires destroyed or greatly altered much of the pineland as well as the cypress strands in 1962 and 1965. Epiphytes, orchids, and bromeliads are abundant. Many grassy prairies break up the woodlands. These prairies are perpetuated by fires.

Plant Associations

The principal plant associations of the Big Cypress are quite similar to those described in other provinces but some have distinctive features associated with the more sandy soil with lower pH values as well as the presence of several plant species not found in other provinces. In addition, some plants, such as pop ash and water oak, occur here in greater abundance.

Ponds in the Big Cypress are shallow, formed in depressions of the bedrock in contrast to those found in Provinces IV and V. Practically all the associations found here are described in the treatment of Provinces IV, V, VI, and VIII, including Dwarf Cypress, Pop Ash Heads, and Custard Apple Swamps. An additional eleven associations are described: Palmetto Savannah, Cypress Forests, Dwarf Cypress, Pine Islands, Bay Heads, Tropical Hardwood Hammocks, Gum Slough, Coastal Sand Dunes and Shell Mounds, Sand Scrub, Pine Flatwoods, and Prairies.

Palmetto Savannah

Palmetto is widespread throughout this province. It is usually in scattered clumps or mixed with pine or cypress. (See p. 131.) Near the boundary of the Freshwater Swamps and the Big Cypress some large clumps of palmetto covering several acres are found. Some of these are almost pure stands built up on 2 to 3 feet of peaty soils. Although cabbage palm is much more conspicuous in Collier and western Monroe counties than in Dade County, it appears to be declining in several plant communities.

Cypress Forests

The cypress forests, strands, domes, and scrub probably form 50 percent of the ground cover of this province; at least, flying low over the area gives one this impression. The 1954 soil survey (Leighty, 1954) states that about 85 percent of the land in Collier County is woodland. The Tamiami limestone is less porous than that of the Miami oolite and the Bryozoan limestone of Dade County. It contains much more sand, which settles in the sloughs and basins as the surface rock disintegrates. The soils are slightly more acid, which may promote better growth of the cypress trees. The low relief and ponded structure of most of this topography permits the retention of rainfall throughout much of the year and satisfies the requirements for the survival of cypress seedlings and other swamp trees.

The largest cypress strand (about 2 by 18 miles), the Fahkahatchee, is a composite of several associations, including ponds, prairies, and hammocks on built-up peat supporting tropical hardwoods and large royal palms. This stand of royal palms is the finest remaining in the three-county area. In the slough proper the best development of cypress in

South Florida existed prior to its logging (from 1920 to 1950). The writer spent considerable time in the 1940s in this strand while it was being logged. The common practice in logging large (3 to 6 feet) cypress trees was to kill them by girdling the base several months before felling. This greatly reduced the moisture content in the trunk, lowering the specific gravity to such an extent that the logs floated. Thus they could be more readily dragged across the flooded swamp to the logging railroad. The girdled trees were heavily attacked by ambrosia beetles in the spring, which caused severe degrading of the lumber. Experimental girdling each month of the year indicated that late summer treatment reduced moisture through the winter period when the beetles were inactive, and this resulted in much less damage.

At the extreme southern edge of this slough a section known as the Norris Tract has not been harvested and is still protected by the owner, Mr. Lester J. Norris who lives in nearby Naples. It has been designated as a Natural History Landmark by the National Park Service. Other large sloughs or strands in the area include the Kissimmee, Billy, Camp Kensis, Wilson, Bird, Rookery, Corkscrew, Marsh, and Okaloacoochee.

The soils in these strands may be as much as 6 feet deep. The top 1 to 4 feet consists of muck or brown peat, and the remainder to bedrock is fine sand stained by organic matter.

Vegetation. In addition to the bay head species previously listed for Province IV, a few additional trees are present or more abundant here: water oak, ash, Virginia willow, pop ash, maple, stiff cornel, paurotis palm, nest fern, water lettuce, and lizard tail. The Fahkahatchee and other cypress strands in Collier and western Monroe counties are rich in orchids and bromeliads. In fact, a number of species growing here are not found elsewhere in the United States (Buswell, 1937; Craighead, 1964).

Dwarf Cypress

This association probably occupies a greater area in this province than any other plant community. Here, as in Province IV, the dwarfing reflects the shallow marl soil, which is often only 4 to 10 inches deep with little humus. Fires rarely destroy these trees, as there is not sufficient organic matter to maintain a hot fire.

Pine Islands

Dade County pine extends throughout Collier and western Monroe counties on the better drained outcrops of limestone and on some of the higher, sandy soils. These islands are scattered and usually difficult to approach for logging, although much of the pine has been cut for local use. Quite often cypress in the potholes of the limestone forms a considerable mixture with the pine. The pines grow rapidly and reach greater size than those in Dade County. One of the largest stands seen by the writer is Big Pine Island, which lies just south of the west end of the Loop Road and north of Gum Slough.

Bay Heads

The bay heads of the Big Cypress are not such distinct entities as those in Provinces IV and VII. The swamp trees of these communities push into the margins of the cypress sloughs and the perimeter of the pine islands and hammocks. Water oak, maple, and stiff cornell are abundant.

Tropical Hardwood Hammocks

Hammocks are best developed in the eastern part of this province around Pinecrest. Some are very large (as much as 50 acres), and most of the tropical hardwoods common to the hammocks of the Pineland Ridge of Dade County are represented. Simpson's eugenia and twinberry are abundant; vine fern and air plants tend to be much more numerous in these apparently more humid environments. A thick bed of sandy peat covers the bedrock in these hammocks.

Gum Slough

About 3 miles south of the western end of the Loop Road in Monroe County where the rocky outcrops break off to meet the marl glades of the Freshwater Swamps (Province IV), there is a well-formed gully with a distinct change in vegetation. This area is known as the Gum Slough.

This slough runs across the main drainage from Big Pine Island slightly north of west to where it merges into the scrub mangroves. Why the name Gum Slough was applied here is not known; three visits by the writer into this slough failed to reveal any of the several gum trees found just north of Collier County.

Vegetation. This slough is bordered by a series of hammocks on the higher north side and a mixture of various swamp trees and very tall saw grass in the slough proper. In the western end, red mangrove has penetrated several miles into the slough.

On the rim hammocks the important trees include live oak, marlberry, myrsine, lancewood, gray twig, two species of wild coffee, velvetleaf, dove plum, white stopper, twinberry, black ironwood, mastic, gumbo-limbo, and randia. Lysiloma was not found. The slough also carried the usual swamp hardwoods including water oak, pop ash, maple, and pond apple.

Coastal Sand Dunes and Shell Mounds

Beginning at the north end of the Ten Thousand Islands and extending across Collier County are large mounds of sand and shell. Coastal sand dunes, shell mounds, and mangroves blend into one another in this area. Many are stratified with beds of Indian soil and broken shell. This formation continues on north through Cape Romano, Marco, and Naples, forming a series of dunes several miles wide and 6 to 15 feet high, though occasionally one may reach 50 feet. Apparently these elevations were formed when the sea was much higher. Recent hurricanes have formed new dunes 6 feet in elevation. Some storms deposited over a foot of sand and shell on top of the coastal dunes already 12 feet or more in elevation. Construction work in the Naples area has revealed remains of cypress forests buried under 5 feet of sand.

The coastal dunes taper inland into the cypress swamps 10 to 15 miles and extend to bedrock 6 to 25 feet below. The freshwater aquifer within these sand hills provides the water supply for several coastal towns. These coastal communities could well be considered a distinct province, but wherever a creek crosses them, a bay develops inland, and stands of large mangroves occur.

Vegetation. The vegetation of the coastal dunes is quite variable. Sand-scrub vegetation often occupies much of these hills as well as the very fine sand flats. In places where a peaty soil has formed, swamp hardwoods may be present. Good stands of Dade County pine were once common on these sands. Several characteristic plants of the dunes proper are reindeer moss, spike moss, live oak, hog plum, gallberry, prickly pears, staggerbush, periwinkle, yellow allamanda, saltbush, palafoxia, avocado, banana, and scrub oak.

Sand Scrub

Wedged between the sand hills of the west coast and the cypress swamps are small areas of several acres of deep white to gray, fine sands of the St. Lucie and Lakewood soil types (Leighty et al., 1964). Several occur in the vicinity of Naples. These are sands of very low fertility, excessively drained, bearing a scrubby vegetation locally known as "the scrub" (Harper, 1927). The sand is very difficult to sample

Sand scrub. *Areas of scrub are rather small and scattered, usually lying on or between sand dunes. Sand pine (not shown), scrub oak, and rosemary are characteristic plants.*

with a soil auger or coring tube. When dry it continually fills into the hole, and when wet it holds the instrument so firmly that its withdrawal is difficult. Laessle (1967) suggested that this community formed on old lake beds of Miocene age and that it has existed, with the help of fire, practically unchanged for centuries.

Vegetation. The vegetation is rather open and scattered, although some species such as the oaks and myrtles do form dense thickets. The more common species of trees are sand pine, sand live oak, laurel oak, and dahoon holly; the shrubs include rosemary, wax myrtle, gallberry, huckleberry, dwarf myrtle, pawpaws, staggerbush, hog plum, Befaria, and saw palmetto.

Pine Flatwoods

The pine flatwoods which occur over several thousand square miles in central and southern Florida on each side of the central highlands extend into northern Collier County. In this province this plant association occurs on poorly drained, fine, sandy soils of the Broward, Charlotte, and Copeland types. The forest cover is chiefly slash pine, which forms very open stands with little underbrush except for extensive mats of saw palmetto, huckleberry, gallberry, pawpaw, rosemary, and wax myrtle.

Prairies

Much of the ground cover of Collier County is made up of ponds and prairies. Often the ponds of the rainy season are the prairies of the dry periods. Most of these prairies appear to be perpetuated by frequent fires that keep down the shrubs and trees. Usually the soil is shallow marl or sand of various particle size, permeability, acidity, and depth, sometimes only thinly covering the limestone. On the basis of these characteristics they have been separated into a number of soil types, and described and named by agronomists (Leighty, 1965). Many of these soils have been tested for agriculture, but the only large-scale use is on the fine sands of the Copeland, Keri, Broward, Matmon, and Suniland types. Very little timber land has been cleared for farming here.

Vegetation. Saw grass is a common component where the

soils are deeper, as along the margins of the sloughs. The prairies that tend to hold water most of the year carry both submerged and emergent vegetation. On those sites draining more quickly, grasses predominate. Some of the more common submerged plants are bladderwort, bonnets, water lilies, and floating heart. The emergent plants are pickerelweed, arrowhead, maiden cane, saw grass, beard grass, spike rushes, and cattails. The drier prairies support broom sedges, white top sedges, switch grass, saw palmetto, pawpaw, gallberry, and foxtail grass.

substrate: underlying or basal structure

swash line: ridge of debris left inland by the farthest reach of the swash, or mass of rushing water, after a storm

taproot: the primary descending root; a continuation of a stem

tolerant: the ability of some trees to grow in the understory in varying degrees of shade; also, salt-tolerant, etc.

transpiration: the emission of watery vapor from leaves or other parts of plants

windthrow: uprooting by wind

xerophitic: having low moisture requirements

Selected References

Books

Barbour, Thomas. *That Vanishing Eden, A Naturalist's Florida.* New York: G. P. Putnam's Sons, 1944.

Chapman, V. J. *Salt Marshes and Salt Deserts of the World.* New York: Interscience Publishers, Inc., 1960.

Craighead, Frank C. *Orchids and Other Air Plants of the Everglades National Park.* Coral Gables, Fla.: Univ. of Miami Press, 1963.

Dodd, Dorothy. *Florida, The Land of Romance.* Tallahassee: Florida Department of Agriculture, 1956.

Dunn, Gordon E., and Miller, Banner I. *Atlantic Hurricanes.* Rev. ed. Baton Rouge: Louisiana State Univ. Press, 1964.

Fontaneda, Hernando d'Escalante. *Memoir of D^O . d'Escalante Fontaneda Respecting Florida.* Spain, ca. 1575. Tr. by Buckingham Smith, Washington, D.C., 1854. Reprinted with revisions, David O. True, ed. Miami: Univ. of Miami and Historical Assn. of Southern Florida, 1944.

Gifford, John C. *Living by the Land.* Coral Gables, Fla.: Glade House, 1945.

Heilprin, A. *Exploration of the West Coast of Florida and in the Okeechobee Wilderness.* Philadelphia, 1887.

Kurz, Herman, and Godfrey, Robert K., with the collaboration of Kenneth E. Wagner. *Trees of Northern Florida.* Gainesville: Univ. of Florida Press, 1962.

McIlhenny, E. A. *The Alligator's Life History.* Boston: Christopher Publishing House, 1935.

Meunscher, W. C. *Aquatic Plants of the United States.* Ithaca, N.Y.: Comstock Publishing Co., Inc., 1944.

Simpson, Charles Torrey. *Florida Wild Life.* New York: Macmillan and Co., 1932.

Simpson, Charles Torrey. *In Lower Florida Wilds*. New York: G. P. Putnam's Sons, 1920.

Simpson, Charles Torrey. *Out of Doors in Florida*. Miami: E. B. Douglas Co., 1923.

Small, John Kunkel. *Ferns of the Southeastern United States*. Darien, Conn.: Hafner Publishing Co., 1938.

Small, John Kunkel. *Manual of the Southeastern Flora*. Chapel Hill: Univ. of North Carolina Press, 1933.

Strogonov, B. P. *Physiological Basis of Salt Tolerance in Plants*. Tr. from the Russian, published by Israel Program for Scientific Translations. New York: Daniel Davey & Co., 1962.

U.S. Forest Service. *Woody Plant Manual*. U.S. Department of Agriculture, Misc. Pub. No. 654. Washington, D.C., 1948.

Willoughby, Hugh L. *Across the Everglades: A Canoe Journey of Exploration*. Philadelphia: J. B. Lippincott Co., 1898.

Articles and Reports

Ahlgren, I. F., and Ahlgren, C. E. "Ecological Effects of Forest Fires." *Botanical Review* 26 (1960):483-553.

Alexander, Taylor R. "Effects of Hurricane Betsy on the Southeastern Everglades." *Florida Academy of Sciences. Quarterly Journal* 30 (No. 1, 1967).

Alexander, Taylor R. "Observations on the Ecology of the Low Hammocks of Southern Florida." *Florida Academy of Sciences. Quarterly Journal* 18 (1955).

Alexander, Taylor R. "Plant Succession on Key Largo, Florida, involving *Pinus caribaea* and *Quercus virginiana*." *Florida Academy of Sciences. Quarterly Journal* 16 (1953):133-138.

Alexander, Taylor R. "A Tropical Hammock on the Miami (Florida) Limestone." *Ecology* 48 (No. 5, 1967):863-867.

Allen, Philip E. "Ecological Bases for Land Use Planning in the Gulf Coast Marshland." *Journal of Soil and Water Conservation* 5 (1950):57-62.

Allison, R. V. "The Influence of Drainage and Cultivation on Subsidence of Organic Soils Under Conditions of Everglades Reclamation." *Proceedings of the Soil and Crop Science of Florida* 16 (1956).

Bartach, Paul. "An Ecological Cross-section of the Lower Part of Florida Based Largely upon its Molluscan Fauna." Washington, D.C., Smithsonian Institution, Report of the Committee on Paleoecology, 1936.

Beard, Daniel B., and Weber, W. A. "Wildlife of the Everglades National Park." *National Geographic Magazine* XCV (No. 1, 1949):83-116.

Beard, J. S. "Climax Vegetation in Tropical America." *Ecology* 25 (No. 2, 1944):127-158.

Bernstein, Leon. "Salt Tolerance of Plants." Washington, D.C., U.S. Dept. of Agriculture, Agricultural Information Bulletin No. 283, 1964.

Bessey, E. A. "The Hammocks and Everglades of Southern Florida." *Plant World* 14 (1911):268-276.

Bowman, H. H. M. "The Ecology and Physiology of the Red Mangrove." *Proceedings of the American Philosophical Society* 56 (1917):589-672.

Buswell, Walter M. "Orchids of the Big Cypress." *American Journal of Botany* 43 (1937):147-153.

Butson, K. D., and Prine, G. M. "Weekly Rainfall Frequencies in Florida." Gainesville, Fla., Agricultural Experiment Station, Circular S-187, 1968.

Chamberlain, E. B., Jr. "Florida Waterfront Populations, Habitats and Management." Tallahassee, Fla., Game and Fresh Water Fish Commission, Technological Bulletin No. 7, 1960.

Craighead, Frank C. "Land, Mangroves, and Hurricanes." *Fairchild Tropical Garden Bulletin* 19 (No. 4, 1964).

Craighead, Frank C. "The Mangrove Belt of Southern Florida Including the Ten Thousand Islands." Mimeographed. Presented at Hearing of the Collier County Commission considering urbanization of the Ten Thousand Islands, April 7, 1967.

Craighead, Frank C. "The Role of the Alligator in Shaping Plant Communities and Maintaining Wildlife in the Southern Everglades." *Florida Naturalist* 41 (Nos. 1, 2, 1968).

Craighead, Frank C. "Two Mysteries of the Everglades," *Florida Naturalist* 17(No. 2, 1970):38.

Craighead, Frank C. "Vegetation and Recent Sedimentation in the Everglades National Park." *Florida Naturalist* 42 (No. 4, 1969).

Craighead, Frank C., and Gilbert, V. C. "The Effect of Hurricane Donna on the Vegetation of South Florida." *Florida Academy of Sciences. Quarterly Journal* 25 (No. 1, 1962).

Dalton, J. D. "Salt Line Reports." Mimeographed. Homestead, Fla., Agricultural Extension Service, 1965-1969.

Davis, John H., Jr. "The Ecology and Geologic Role of Mangroves in Florida." Washington, D.C., Carnegie Institution, Publication No. 517, 1940.

Davis, John H., Jr. "The Natural Features of Southern Florida." Tallahassee, Fla., Dept. of Conservation, Geological Survey Bulletin No. 25, 1943.

Davis, John H., Jr. "The Peat Deposits of Florida." Tallahassee, Fla., Geological Survey, Bulletin 30, 1946.

Davis, John H., Jr. "Vegetation of the Everglades and Conservation From the Point of View of the Ecologist." *Soil Science Society of Florida. Proceedings.* Vol. A-105-115, 1943.

Demaree, Delzie. "Submerging Experiments with Taxodium." *Ecology* 13 (1932):258-261.

Eggler, Willis A., and Russell, R. J., eds. "Louisiana Coastal Marsh Ecology." Baton Route, Louisiana State Univ., Coastal Studies Institute, Technical Report No. 14, 1961.

Egler, Frank E. "Mahogany: A Potential Resource of South Florida." *Journal of Forestry* 39 (No. 8, 1941).

Egler, Frank E. "Southeast Saline Everglades; Vegetation of Florida, and Its Management." *Vegetatio Acta Botanica* III (Fasc. 4-5, 1932):213-265.

Ford, Robert N. "The Everglades Agricultural Area." Univ. of Chicago, Dept. of Geography, Research Paper No. 42, 1956.

"Forest Cover Types of North America." Washington, D.C., Society of American Foresters, Report of the Committee on Forest Types, 1954.

Gallatin, M. H., et al. "Soil Survey of Dade County, Florida." Washington, D.C., U.S. Dept. of Agriculture and Florida Agricultural Experiment Station, 1958.

Gifford, John C. "Florida Keys, Soil Productivity." Tallahassee, Fla., Dept. of Agriculture, New Series No. 77, 1946.

Gifford, John C. "Southern Florida. Notes on the Forest Conditions of the Southernmost Part of this Remarkable Peninsula." *Forestry and Irrigation* (Sept., 1904).

Ginsburg, R. N. "Environmental Relationships of Grain Size and Constituent Particles in Some South Florida Carbonate Sediments." *American Assn. of Petroleum Geologists. Bulletin* 40 (No. 10, 1956).

Ginsburg, R. N. "The Influence of Marine Bottom Communities on the Depositional Environment of Sediments." *Journal of Geology* 66 (1958).

Ginsburg, R. N., et al. "South Florida Carbonate Sediments." Tallahassee, Fla., State Geological Survey, Guide Book No. 1, for Geological Society of America meeting in Miami, 1964.

Gunn, Charles R. "Stranded Seeds and Fruits from the Southeastern

Shore of Florida." *Garden Journal of the New York Botanical Garden* 18 (No. 2, 1968).

Gunter, Gordon. "The Water Needs of the Everglades National Park. Some Relations of Estaurine Organisms to Salinity." Mimeographed. From *Limnology and Oceanography* 6 (No. 2, 1967).

Harlow, Richard F., and Jones, F. K., Jr. "The White-tailed Deer in Florida." Tallahassee, Fla., Game and Fresh Water Fish Commission, Technological Bulletin No. 9, 1965.

Harper, R. M. " 'Hammock,' 'Hommock' or 'Hummock'? " *Science* 22 (1905):400-402.

Harper, R. M. "Natural Resources of Southern Florida." Tallahassee, Fla., State Geological Survey, 18th Annual Report, 1927, pp. 25-206.

Harper, R. M. "Some Vanishing Scenic Features of the Southeastern United States." *Natural History* 19 (No. 2, 1919):192-204.

Hartwell, J. H. "Some Aspects of the Availability of Water in the Everglades, Florida." Mimeographed. Tallahassee, Fla., U.S. Geological Survey in cooperation with the National Park Service, October, 1968.

Hartwell, J. H.; Klein, H.; and Joyner, B. F. "Preliminary Evaluation of the Hydrologic Situation in the Everglades National Park." Mimeographed. Washington, D.C., U.S. Geological Survey, 1963.

Harshberger, J. W. "The Vegetation of South Florida, South of 27°30' North, Exclusive of the Florida Keys." *Transactions of Wagner Free Institute of Science.* Philadelphia, 1914.

Hela, I. "Remarks on the Climate of Southern Florida." *Bulletin of Marine Science of the Gulf and Caribbean* 2 (No. 2):438-447.

Henderson, J. R. "The Soils of Florida." Gainesville, Fla., Univ. of Florida Agricultural Experiment Station, Bulletin 334, 1939.

Hilman, J. B., and Lewis, C. E. "Effect of Burning on South Florida Range." Washington, D.C., U.S. Dept. of Agriculture, Southeastern Forest Experiment Station, Paper 146, 1962.

Hoffmeister, J. E.; Stockman, K. W.; and Multer, H. G. "Miami Limestone of Florida and Its Recent Bahamian Counterpart." *Geological Society of America Bulletin* 78 (1967):175-190.

Holdridge, L. R. "Some Notes on the Mangrove Swamps of Puerto Rico." *Caribbean Forester* 1 (No. 1, 1940).

Hordon, Robert M. "Land Use in the Florida Everglades." Master's thesis, Univ. of Chicago, 1965.

Johnson, Lamar. "A Survey of the Water Resources of the Everglades National Park." Mimeographed. Report to the Superintendent, Everglades National Park, 1958.

Jones, L. A. "Soils, Geology, and Water Control in the Everglades." Washington, D.C., U.S. Dept. of Agriculture, Soil Conservation Service, Agricultural Experiment Station, Bulletin 442, 1948.

Klein, Howard, and Sherwood, C. B. "Hydrologic Conditions in the Vicinity of Levee 30, Northern Dade County, Florida." Tallahassee, Fla., State Geological Survey, 1961.

Kurz, Herman. "Florida Dunes and Scrub Vegetation and Geology." Tallahassee, Fla., State Geological Survey, Bulletin 23, 1942.

Laessle, A. M. "Relationship of Sand Pine Scrub to Former Shore Lines." *Florida Academy of Sciences. Quarterly Journal* 30 (No. 4, 1967).

Langdon, D. Gordon. "Silvicultural Characteristics of Bald Cypress." Asheville, N.C., Southeastern Forest Experiment Station, Paper No. 94, 1968.

Leighty, Ralph G., et al. "Soil Survey of Collier County, Florida." Washington, D.C., U.S. Dept. of Agriculture and Fla. Agricultural Experiment Station, 1964.

Llewellyn, W. R. "Some Soil Associations in the Mangrove Region of the Everglades National Park." Mimeographed. Report for Everglades National Park, June, 1967.

Loveless, C. M. "The Everglades Deer Herd, Life History and Management." Tallahassee, Fla., Game and Fresh Water Fish Commission, Technical Bulletin No. 6, 1959.

Loveless, C. M. "A Study of the Vegetation in the Florida Everglades." *Ecology* 40 (No. 1, 1959).

MacGregor, William H. "Flatwoods Farms; Woodlot Improvement Pays." Gainesville, Univ. of Florida Agricultural Extension Service, Circular 125, 1954.

Mader, Donald L., and Lull, Howard W. "Depth, Weight, and Water Storage of the Forest Floor in White Pine Stands in Massachusetts." Washington, D.C., U.S. Forest Service, Research Paper NE-109, 1968.

Mattoon, Wilbur R. "The Southern Cypress." Washington, D.C., U.S. Dept. of Agriculture, Bulletin 272, 1915.

Mattoon, Wilbur R. "Water Requirements and Growth of Young Cypress." *Proceedings of the Society of American Foresters* 11 (1916):192-197.

Meskimen, George F. "Melaleuca." Master's thesis, Univ. of Florida, School of Forestry, 1960.

Monroe, Watson H. "Formation of Tropical Karst Topography by Limestone Solution and Reprecipitation." *Caribbean Journal of Science* 6 (Nos. 1, 2, 1966).

Morgan, James P. "Coastal Morphological Changes Resulting from Hurricane Audrey." Athens, Univ. of Georgia, Marine Institute, 1959.

Odum, E. P. "The Role of Tidal Marshes in Estaurine Production." Contribution No. 29 from Univ. of Georgia Marine Institute. Reprinted, *New York State Conservationist,* June-July, 1961.

Parker, G. G., and Cooke, C. Wythe. "Late Cenozoic Geology of Southern Florida." Tallahassee, Fla., State Geological Survey, Geological Bulletin No. 27, 1944.

Parker, C. G., et al. "Water Resources of Southern Florida with Special Reference to Geology and Ground Water of the Miami Area." Washington, D.C., U.S. Geological Survey, Water Supply Paper 1255, 1955.

Pearson, G. A. "Tolerance of Crops to Exchangable Sodium." Washington, D.C., U.S. Dept. of Agriculture, Agricultural Research Service, Agricultural Information Bulletin No. 216, 1960.

Perkins, R. C., and Enos, Paul. "Hurricane Betsy in the Florida-Bahama Area." *Journal of Geology* 76 (1968):710-717.

Philips, Walter S. "A Tropical Hammock on the Miami (Fla.) Limestone." *Ecology* 21 (No. 2, 1940):165-175.

Phillips, O. P. "Recent Sedimentary Record in Mangrove Swamps and Rise in Sea Level over the Southwestern Coast of Florida." In *Marine Geology,* Elseiver Publishing Co., Amsterdam, Netherlands, 1964.

Phillips, O. P. "The Geology and Sedimentology of Mangrove Swamps." In *Encyclopedia of Earth Science.* R. W. Fairbridge, ed., Reinhold Publishing Co., N.Y., 1965.

Phliger, Fred B. "Sedimentary Environments in a Salt Marsh." *Science* 154 (Dec. 23, 1966).

Provost, Maurice W. "Florida Estuaries and Their Protection." Mimeographed. State Board of Health, Vero Beach, Fla., 1968.

Provost, Maurice W. "Impounding Salt Marshes for Mosquito Control and Its Effect on Florida Bird Life." *Florida Naturalist* 32 (No. 4, 1959).

Puri, Harbons S., and Vernon, Robert O. "Summary of the Geology of Florida and a Guide Book to the Classic Exposures." Tallahassee, Fla., State Geological Survey, Special Publication No. 5, 1964.

Redfield, Alfred C. "Ontogeny of a Salt Marsh Estuary." *Science* 147 (Jan. 1, 1965).

Redford, Polly. "Our Vanishing Tidelands." *Readers Digest,* September, 1967; reprinted from *Atlantic Monthly,* June, 1967.

Richards, L. A. "Availability of Water to Crops on Saline Soils." Washington, D.C., U.S. Dept. of Agriculture, Information Bulletin No. 210, 1959.

Robertson, William B., Jr. "Everglades Fires—Past, Present and Future."*Everglades Natural History Magazine* 2 (No. 1, 1954).

Ruehle, George D. "Grafted Casuarina Trees for Use as Windbreaks or Ornamentals." *Proceedings of the Florida State Horticultural Society,* pp. 199-201, November, 1952.

Russell, R. J., and Morgan, James P. "Louisiana's Changing Shore-lines." Baton Rouge, Louisiana State Univ., Coastal Studies Institute. Technical Report No. 20, Part A, 1963.

Sass, Louis C. "Rainfall Distribution in the Miami Area." *Florida Academy of Sciences. Quarterly Journal* 30 (No. 2, 1967).

Scholl, David W. "High Interstitial Water Chlorinity in Estuarine Mangrove Swamps, Florida." *Nature* 207 (No. 4994, July 17, 1965):284-285.

Scholl, David W.; Craighead, F. C.; and Stuiver, Minze. "Florida Submergence Curve Revised: Its Relation to Coastal Sedimentation Rates." *Science* 163 (Feb., 1969):562-564.

Scholl, David W., and Stuiver, Minze. "Recent Submergence of Southern Florida." *Geological Society of America Bulletin* 78 (April, 1967):437-454.

Scholl, David W., and Taft, William H. "Algae, Contributors to the Formation of Calcareous Tufa, Mono Lake, California." *Journal of Sedimentary Petrology* 34 (No. 2, 1964):309-319.

Small, John Kunkel. For a selected chronological listing of some of this prolific author's publications pertinent to this volume *see* pp. 194-197.

Smith, Hugh M. "Notes on Biscayne Bay, Florida," Washington, D.C., Report of the Commissioners of Fish and Fisheries of 1896, Appendix 2.

Smith, R. H. "Management of Salt Marshes on the Atlantic Coast of the United States." Transactions of the 7th North American Wildlife Conference, pp. 272-277, 1942.

Smith, William H. Urbana, Illinois, State Geological Survey. Personal communication, December 18, 1964.

Spackman, W.; Dolson, C. P.; and Reigel, W. "Phytogenic Organic Sediments and Sedimentary Environments in the Everglades Mangrove Complex." *Palaeontographica* Abt. B 117 (1966): 135-152.

Stockman, K. W.; Ginsburg, R. N.; and Shinn, E. A. "The Production of Lime Mud by Algae in South Florida." *Journal of Sedimentary Petrology* 37 (No. 2, 1967).

Tabb, Durbin C. "A Summary of Existing Information on the Fresh-water, Brackish Water and Marine Ecology of the Florida Everglades Region in Relation to Fresh-water Needs of Everglades National Park." Mimeographed report. Coral Gables, Fla., Univ. of Miami Institute of Marine Sciences, 1963.

Tabb, Durbin C.; Durbrow, D. L.; and Manning, Raymond B. "The Ecology of Northern Florida Bay and Adjacent Estuaries." Tallahassee, Fla., Board of Conservation, Technical Series 39, pp. 1-79, 1962.

Tabb, Durbin C., and Jones, A. C. "Effect of Hurricane Donna on the Aquatic Fauna of North Florida Bay." *American Fisheries Society. Transactions* 91 (No. 4, 1962):375-378.

Tabb, Durbin C., and Manning, Raymond B. "A Checklist of the Flora and Fauna of Northern Florida Bay and Adjacent Brackish Waters of the Florida Mainland." *Bulletin of Marine Science of the Gulf and Caribbean* 11 (No. 4, 1961):552-649.

Taft, William H., and Harbaugh, John W. "Modern Carbonate Sediments of Southern Florida, the Bahamas, and Espiritu Santo Island, Baja, California." Stanford, Cal., Stanford Univ., Geological Sciences Misc. Pub., Vol. 8, No. 2, 1964.

Taylor, William Randolph. "Sketch of the Character of the Marine Algal Vegetation of the Shores of the Gulf of Mexico." In *Gulf of Mexico, Its Origin, Waters, and Marine Life.* Washington, D.C., U.S. Dept. of the Interior, Fish and Wildlife Service, Fishery Bulletin 89, 1954.

Thorne, Robert F. "Flowering Plants of the Waters and Shores of the Gulf of Mexico." In *Gulf of Mexico, Its Origin, Waters, and Marine Life.* Washington, D.C., U.S. Dept. of the Interior, Fish and Wildlife Service, Fishery Bulletin 89, 1954.

Trask, Parker D. "Additional Notes to E. M. Thorpe, Florida and Bahama Marine Calcareous Deposits In Recent Marine Sediments." Tulsa, Okla., American Assn. of Petroleum Geologists, 1939; reprinted, 1955.

Uhler, F. M. "Control of Undesirable Plants in Waterfall Habitats." Transactions of the 9th North American Wildlife Conference, pp. 295-303, 1944.

Uphof, J. C. T. "The Plant Formations of the Coral Reefs Along the Northern Coast of Cuba." *American Journal of Botany* 11 (1924):409-416.

Vernon, Robert O. "Cypress Domes." *Science* 105 (No. 2717, January 24, 1947).

Wadsworth, Frank H. "Growth and Regeneration of White Mangrove in Puerto Rico." *Caribbean Forester* 20 (Nos. 3, 4, 1959).

Wadsworth, Frank H., and Englerth, George H. "Effects of the 1956 Hurricane on Forests in Puerto Rico." *Caribbean Forester* 20 (Nos. 1, 2, 1959):38.

"Waterfowl Tomorrow." Washington, D.C., U.S. Dept. of the Interior, 1964.

Wells, B. W. "A New Forest Climax Salt Spray, Smith Island, N.C." *Torrey Botanical Club. Bulletin* 66:629-634.

Wells, B. W., and Shunk, I. V. "Salt Spray, An Important Factor in Coastal Ecology." *Torrey Totanical Club. Bulletin* 65:485-492.

Wells, Philip V. "Scarp Woodlands, Transported Grassland Soils, and Concept of Grassland Climate in the Great Plains Region." *Science* 148 (April 9, 1965).

Whittaker, R. H. "A Consideration of Climax Theory: The Climax as a Population and Pattern." *Ecological Monographs* 23 (1953):41-78.

Will, Lawrence E. "Digging the Cape Sable Canal." *Tequesta* 19 (1959).

Young, F. N. "Fire in the 'Glades.' " *Everglades Natural History Magazine* 2 (No. 2, 1954):25-29.

Zimmermann, M. H.; Waldrop, A. B.; and Tomlinson, P. B. "Tension Wood in Aerial Roots of the *Ficus benjamina* L." *Wood Science and Technology* 2 (1968):95-104.

Selected References by John Kunkel Small

The works of John Kunkel Small have been a basic source of information for botanists working in the Southeast. His two major books (*Manual of the Southeastern Flora,* 1933 and *Ferns of the Southeastern States,* 1938) gave comprehensive treatment to most of the plants of the region. In addition, he published several hundred papers and scientific reports. While many of the scientific names he employed are now obsolete, his works are frequently cited and are used extensively by modern scientists.

A selection of his articles pertaining to this volume are listed here; another list dealing with specific trees of the region will be included in Volume II of *Trees of South Florida.*

1907a "Exploration of Southern Florida." *Garden Journal of the New York Botanical Garden* 8 (February):23-28.

1907b "Explorations in Southern Florida." Abstract, in *Torreya* 7 (April 15):83-84.

1907c   "Additions to the Tree Flora of the United States." *Torreya* 7 (June 19):123-125.

1909a   "Exploration in the Everglades." *Garden Journal of the New York Botanical Garden* 10 (March):48-55.

1909b   "Exploration in the Everglades." Abstract in *Torreya* 9 (April 30):100-103.

1911   "Exploration in Southern Florida." *Garden Journal of the New York Botanical Garden* 12 (July):147-156.

1914   "Exploration in the Everglades and on the Florida Keys." *Garden Journal of the New York Botanical Garden* 15 (May):69-79; plates 129-131.

1916a   "Royal Palm Hammock." *Garden Journal of the New York Botanical Garden* 16 (November 3):165-172; plates 179-182.

1916b   "A Cruise to the Cape Sable Region of Florida." *Garden Journal of the New York Botanical Garden* 17 (November 20):189-202; plates 183-188.

1916c   "Exploration in Southern Florida in 1915." *Garden Journal of the New York Botanical Garden* 17 (April 3):37-45; plates 166-168.

1917   "Botanical Exploration in Southern Florida in 1916." *Garden Journal of the New York Botanical Garden* 18 (June 11):98-111; plates 195-199.

1919a   "Coastwise Dunes and Lagoons: A Record of Botanical Exploration in Florida in the Spring of 1918." *Garden Journal of the New York Botanical Garden* 20 (November 8):191-207; plates 236-238.

1919b   "Cape Sable Region of Florida." *Garden Journal of the New York Botanical Garden* 20 (December 24): 1-27, illus.

1920a   "Of Grottoes and Ancient Dunes: A Record of Exploration in Florida in December 1918." *Garden Journal of the New York Botanical Garden* 21:25-38; plates 241-242.

1920b   "Cypress and Population in Florida: The Relation of Phytogeography to the Drift of Population as Shown in the Case of Taxodium." *Garden Journal of the New York Botanical Garden* 21 (June 17):81-86; plates 245-247.

1921a   "A Botanical Excursion to the Big Cypress." *Natural History* 20 (February 14):488-500.

1921b   "Old Trails and New Discoveries: A Record of Exploration in Florida in the Spring of 1919." *Garden Journal of the New York Botanical Garden* 22 (March 12):25-40; plates 253-254; concluded (April 14):49-64; plates 255-256.

1922a   "The Botanical Fountain of Youth. A Record of Exploration in Florida in April 1920." *Garden Journal of the New York Botanical Garden* 23:117-133; plates 275-276.

1922b "Wild Pumpkins. Have We Found the Original Home of This Garden Esculent? " *Garden Journal of the New York Botanical Garden* 23: (April 21):19-23.

1923a "Historic Trails, By Land and By Water. A Record of Exploration in Florida in December 1919." *Garden Journal of the New York Botanical Garden* 22 (March 10):193-222; plates 263-266.

1923b "Land of the Question Mark. Report on Exploration in Florida in December 1920." *Garden Journal of the New York Botanical Garden* 24 (February 19):25-43; concluded (March 21):62-70.

1923c "Green Deserts and Dead Gardens. A Record of Exploration in Florida in the Spring of 1921." *Garden Journal of the New York Botanical Garden* 24 (November 10):193-247.

1924a "The Land Where Spring Meets Autumn. A Record of Exploration in Florida in December, 1921." *Garden Journal of the New York Botanical Garden* 25 (March):53-94; plates 285-287.

1924b "The Cacti—An Interesting Plant Group in the Study of Survival." *Garden Journal of the New York Botanical Garden* 25 (July): 197-201.

1926 "Gathering Cacti in the Eastern Coastal Plain. A Record of Botanical Exploration in August, 1922." *Garden Journal of the New York Botanical Garden* 26:241-258; concluded (January 12):265-285.

1928 "Botanical Fields, Historic and Prehistoric. A Record of Exploration in the Southeastern Coastal Plain in the Spring of 1923." *Garden Journal of the New York Botanical Garden* 29 (July):149-179; continued (August):185-209; concluded (September):223-235.

1929 "The Everglades." *Scientific Monthly* 28 (January):80-87.

1930a "The Vegetation and Erosion on the Everglade Keys." *Scientific Monthly* 30 (January):33-49.

1930b "The Okeechobee Gourd *(Pepo okeechobeensis)*." *Garden Journal of the New York Botanical Garden* 31 (January):10-14.

1931a "The Cypress, Southern Remnant of a Northern Fossil Type." *Garden Journal of the New York Botanical Garden* 32 (June):125-135.

1931b "Botanical Crossroads, Historic and Prehistoric." *Garden*

Journal of the New York Botanical Garden 32 (April):92-94. Author's separates contain two full-page figures, omitted in error from the original.

1932a "Cypress Trees and Air-Plants." *Garden Journal of the New York Botanical Garden* 33 (June):117-123.

1932b "Natural Grafts." *Garden Journal of the New York Botanical Garden* 33 (October):213-219.

Index to
Common and Scientific Names

brown fringe rush, *Fimbristylis castanea*
bulrush, three-square, *Scirpus americanus*
bumelia (saffron plum), *Bumelia celastrina*
burreed, *Sparganium americanum*
bustic, *Dipholis salicifolia*
butterfly orchid, *Epidendrum tampense*
buttonbush, *Cephalanthus occidentalis*
buttonwood, *Conocarpus erecta*
cabbage palm, *Sabal palmetto*
cactus, Cactaceae family, many spp.
cajeput, *Melaleuca leucadendra*
caper, bay-leaved, *Capparis flexuosa* Jamaica, *C. cynophallophora*
capraria (twinflower), *Capraria biflora*
careless, *Acnida cuspidata*
casuarina (Australian pine), *Casuarina equisetifolia*
catopsis, yellow, *Catopsis berteroniana*
catsclaw, *Pithecellobium unguis-cati*
cattails, Typha spp.
century plant, *Agave decipens*
Cherokee bean, *Erythrina herbacea*
chicken grape, *Vitis rotundifolia*
chloris (finger grasses), Chloris spp.
Christmasberry, *Lycium carolinianum*
cinnamon, wild, *Canella winterana*
cladonia, Cladonia spp.
clusia, *Clusia rosea*
coconut palm (coco palm), *Cocos nucifera*
coco plum, *Chrysobalanus icaco*
colubrinas, Colubrina spp.
coontail, *Ceratophyllus demersum*
coontie (Florida arrowroot), *Zamia integrifolia*
coral beans, Erythrina spp.
cord grass, *Spartina alterniflora*
　beach cord grass, *S. patens*
　big cord grass, *S. cynosuroides*
　prickly cord grass (tall cord grass, switch grass), *S. spartinae*
　sand cord grass, *S. bakeri*
crabwood, *Gymnathes lucida*
crested atriplex, *Atriplex pentandra*
custard apple (pond apple), *Annona glabra*

cypress, bald (dwarf), *Taxodium distichum*
Dade County pine (slash pine), *Pinus elliottii* var *densa*
dahoon holly, *Ilex cassine*
dalbergias (fishpoison vines), Dalbergia spp.
darling plum (red ironwood), *Reynosia septentrionalis*
devil's claw, *Pisonia aculeata*
dildoe, *Acanthocerus floridanus*
dodonea (varnishleaf), *Dodonea microcarya*
dogwood, Jamaica, *Piscidia piscipula*
dollar orchid, *Epidendrum boothianum*
dolls daisy, *Boltonia diffusa*
dove plum (pigeon plum), *Coccoloba diversifolia*
dropseed, *Sporobulus domingensis*
dwarf cypress, *Taxodium distichum*
dwarf myrtle, *Myrica pusilla*
eugenias (stoppers), Eugenia spp.
　red stopper, *E. rhombea*
　Simpson's stopper, *E. simpsonii*
　Spanish stopper, *E. myrtoides*
　twinberry, *E. dicrana*
　white stopper, *E. axillaris*
eupatoriums (thoroughworts), Eupatorium spp.
everglade daisy, *Helenium vernale*
false boxwood (Florida boxwood), *Gyminda latifolia*
fern (s):
　bracken, *Pteridium aquilinum*
　leather, Acrostichum spp.
　ladderbrake, *Pteris vittata*
　nest, *Asplenum serratum*
　pineland, *Anemia adiantifolia*
　swamp, *Blechnum serrulatum*
ficus (figs, banyans), Ficus spp.
fig, strangler, *Ficus aurea*
firegrass, *Andropogon cabonisii*
fishpoison vines, *Dalbergia ecastophyllum, D. amerimnon*
fleabane, *Erigeron quercifolius*
floating heart, *Nymphoides aquatica*
Florida arrowroot (coontie), *Zamia integrifolia*
Florida boxwood (false boxwood), *Gyminda latifolia*
Florida hopbush, *Cupanea glabra*
forestieras, Forestiera spp.
　pineland olive, *F. pinetorum*

wild olive, *F. segregata*
foxtail grasses, Setaria spp.
fringe rush, *Fimbristylus castanea*
frog's-bit, *Limnobium spongia*
gallberry, *Ilex glabra*
geiger tree, *Cordia sebestena*
gerardias, Gerardia spp.
glasswort, *Salicornia perrenis*
goldenrods, Solidago spp.
grape, chicken, *Vitis rotundifolia*
    possum, *Cissus sicyoides*
    sea, *Coccoloba uvifera*
gray twig (schoepfia, whitewood),
    Schoepfia chrysophylloides
great bulrush, *Scirpus validus*
green arum, *Peltandra sagittifolia*
greenbrier, *Smilax laurifolia*
guava, *Psidium guajava*
Guiana plum, *Drypetes lateriflora*
gumbo-limbo, *Bursera simaruba*
gyminda (false boxwood), *Gyminda latifolia*
hackberry, *Celtis laevigata*
hemp vine, *Mikania batatifolia*
hibiscus, Hibiscus spp.
hippocratea, *Hippocratea volubilis*
hog plum, *Ximenia americana*
holly, Brazilian, *Shinus terebinthfolius*
    dahoon, *Ilex cassine*
hopbush, Florida, *Cupania glabra*
horned beak rush, *Rhycospora corniculata*
horned pondweed, *Zannichella palustris*
huckleberry, *Vaccinium myrsinites*
inkwood, *Exothea paniculata*
ironwood, black, *Krugiodendron ferreum*
    red, *Reynosia septentrionalis*
    white, *Schaefferia fruticens*
Jamaica caper, *Capparis cynophallophora*
Jamaica dogwood, *Piscidia piscipula*
joewood, *Jacquinia keyensis*
juncus (black rush), *Juncus roemerianus*
justicia, *Justicia lanceolata*
key grass (tidal grass), *Monanthochloe littoralis*
knotweeds, Polygonum spp.
ladder brake, *Pteris vittata*
lancewood, *Nectandara coriacea*
laurel oak, *Quercus laurifolia*

leather ferns, Acrostichum spp.
lignum vitae, *Guaiacum sanctum*
lippias (frogfruits), Lippia spp.
    matted, *L. nodiflora*
    tall, *L. stoechadifolia*
live oak, *Quercus virginiana*
lizard's-tail, *Saururus cernuus*
lobelias, Lobelia spp.
locustberry, *Byrsonima cuneata*
loosestrife, *Lythrum lineare*
lysiloma (wild tamarind), *Lysiloma bahamensis*
mahogany (madeira), *Swietenia mahogoni*
maiden cane, *Panicum hemitomon*
manatee grass, *Syringodium filiforme*
manchineel, *Hippomanea mancinella*
mangrove, black, *Avidennia nitida*
    red, *Rhizophora mangle*
    white, *Laguncularia racemosa*
mangrove mallow, *Pavonia racemosa*
manisurus (tailgrass), *Manisurus rugosa*
maple, red, *Acer rubrum*
marlberry, *Ardisia escallonoides*
marsh fleabane, *Pluchea foetida*
marsh pink, *Sabatia elliottii*
mastic (wild), *Mastichodendron foetidissimum*
mat grass (coral dropseed), *Sporobulus domingensis*
matted figwort, *Bacopa monnieri*
maytenus, *Maytenus phyllanthoides*
mecardonia, *Mecardonia acuminata*
melaleuca (cajeput), *Melaleuca leucadendra*
mermaid weed, *Proserpinaca platycarpa*
milkbark, *Drypetes diversifolia*
mistletoe, *Phoradendron rubrum*
moonflower, *Calonyction aculeatum*
moonvine, *Calonyction tuba*
morinda (Indian mulberry, yellowroot), *Morinda roioc*
myrsine, *Rapanea guianensis*
myrtle, wax, *Myrica cerifera*
naiads (naias), Najas spp.
nakedwood, *Colubrina reclinata*
necklace pod, *Sophora tomentosa*
nest fern, *Asplenium serratum*
nettles, Boehmeria spp.
nicker bean, *Guilandia crista*
oak, laurel, *Quercus laurifolia*
    live, *Q. virginiana*

sand, *Q. geminata*
water, *Q. nigra*
opuntia (prickly pear), *Opuntia dillenii*
orchid, butterfly, *Epidendrum tampense*
dollar, *E. boothianum*
vine, Vanilla spp.
oxypolis, *Oxypolis filformis*
palafoxias, Palafoxia spp.
palmetto, cabbage, *Sabal palmetto*
saw, *Serenoa repens*
palm, coconut (coco), *Cocos nucifera*
paurotis, *Paurotis wrightii*
royal, *Roystonea regia*
silver, *Coccothrinax argentea*
thatch, *Thrinax microcarpa, T. parviflora*
panic grasses, Panicum spp.
panicum, black, *Panicum condensum*
papaya, *Carica papaya*
paradise tree, *Simarouba glauca*
paurotis palm, *Paurotis wrightii*
pawpaw, *Asimina reticulata*
pepper vine, *Ampelopsis arborea*
periwinkle, *Vinca minor*
persimmon, *Diospyros virginiana*
phragmites (reed), *Phragmites australis*
pickerelweed, *Pontederia lanceolata*
pigeon pea, *Cajanus cajan*
pigeon plum (dove plum), *Coccolobus diversifolia*
pine, Australian, *Casuarina equesetifolia*
pine, Dade County (slash), *Pinus elliottii* var *densa*
longleaf, *P. palustris*
sand, *P. clausa*
slash, *P. elliottii* var *densa*
pineland fern, *Anemia adiantifolia*
pineland olive, *Forestiera pinetorum*
pisonia, *Pisonia rotundata*
plume grass, *Erianthus giganteus*
poison ivy, *Toxicodendron radicans*
poisonwood, *Metopium toxiferum*
pond apple (custard apple), *Annona glabra*
pondweed, *Potamogeton nodosus*
poor-man's-patch, *Mentzelia floridana*
pop ash, *Fraxinus caroliana*
possum grape, *Cissus sicyoides*

potato tree, *Solanum verbascifolium*
prickly pear, *Opuntia dillenii*
primrose willows, Jussiaea spp.
railroad vine, *Ipomoea pes-caprae*
randia (white indigoberry), *Randia aculeata*
red bay, *Persea borbonia*
red ironwood, *Reynosia septentrionalis*
red mangrove, *Rhizophora mangle*
red maple, *Acer rubrum*
red stopper, *Eugenia rhombea*
reddish wild pine, *Tillandsia polystachia*
reed, *Phragmites australis*
reindeer mosses, Cladonia spp.
ribbon lily, *Crinum americanum*
rosemary, *Ceratiola ericoides*
rough leaf, *Guettardia scabra*
royal palm, *Roystonea regia*
rubber vine, *Rhabdadenia biflora*
ruppia (wigeongrass), *Ruppia maritima*
saffron plum, *Bumelia celastrina*
saltbush, *Baccharis halimifolia*
salt grass, *Distichlis spicata*
salt joint grass, *Paspalum vaginatum*
saltwort, *Batis maritima*
samphire, *Philoxerus vermicularis*
sand live oak, *Quercus germinata*
sand pine, *Pinus clausa*
sandspurs (sandburs), Cenchrus spp.
sarcostemma, *Sarcostemma clausa*
satinleaf, *Chrysophyllus olivaeforme*
saw grass, *Cladium jamaicense*
saw palmetto, *Serenoa repens*
sea blite, *Suaeda linearis*
sea daisy (blueweed), *Borrichia frutescens*
sea grape, *Coccoloba uvifera*
sea grass, *Halophila engelmannii*
sea lavender, *Tournefortia gnaphalodes*
sea oats, Uniola spp.
sea purslane, *Sesuvium maritima*
seven-year apple, *Casasia clusifolia*
shortleaf fig, *Ficus laevigata*
shy leaf, *Aeschynomene americana*
silver palm, *Coccothrinax argentea*
Simpson's stopper, *Eugenia simpsonii*
sisal, *Agave sisalina*
slash pine (Dade County pine), *Pinus elliottii* var *densa*

smilax, *Smilax laurifolia*
soapberry, *Sapindus saponaria*
Spanish moss, *Tillandsia usneoides*
Spanish stopper, *Eugenia myrtoides*
spartina (cord grasses), Spartina spp.,
   see cord grass
spatterdock, *Nuphar luteum*
spicewoods, Calypranthes spp.
spider lilies, Hymenocallis spp.
spike moss, *Selaginella armata*
spike rush, *Eleocharis cellulosa*
spilanthes, *Spilanthes repens*
staggerbush, *Lyonia fruticosa*
stiff cornel, *Cornus foemina*
stopper, red, *Eugenia rhombea*
   Simpson's, *E. simpsonii*
   Spanish, *E. myrtoides*
   twinberry, *E. dicrana*
   white, *E. axillaris*
strangler fig, *Ficus aurea*
sugarcane, *Saccharum officinarum*
sumac, *Rhus copallina*
swamp fern, *Blechnum serrulatum*
sweet bay, *Magnolia virginiana*
switch grass (tall cord grass), *Spartina
   spartinae*
tail grass, *Manisurus rugosa*
tall cord grass (switch grass), *Spartina
   spartinae*
tall goldenrod, *Solidago sempervirens*
tall sandspur (sandbur), *Cenchrus
   myosuroides*
tamarind, wild, *Lysiloma bahamensis*
tarflower, *Befaria racemosa*
thatch palms, *Thrinax microcarpa*
   and *T. parviflora*
thoroughworts (boneset), Eupatorium spp.
three-square bulrush, *Scirpus americanus*
tillandsia (air plants), Tillandsia spp.,
   see ball moss, reddish wild pine,
   Spanish moss, twisted air plant
torchwood, *Amyris elemifera*
trema, Trema spp.
turtle grass, *Thallasia testudinum*
twinberry, *Eugenia dicrana*
twinflower, *Capraria biflora*

twisted air plant, *Tillandsia circinata*
typhas (cattails), Typha spp.
varnishleaf (Florida Keys), *Dodonea
   microcarya*
   (mainland), *D. jamaicensis*
velvetleaf (satinleaf), *Chrysophyllum
   olivaeforme*
vine fern, *Vittaria lineota*
vine orchids, Vanilla spp.
Virginia creeper, *Parthenocossus
   quinquefolia*
Virginia willow, *Itea virginica*
water dropwort, *Oxypolis filiformis*
water lettuce, *Pistia strafiotes*
water lily, white, *Nymphaea odorata*
   yellow, *N. mexicana*
water milfoil, *Myriophyllum pinnatum*
water oak, *Quercus nigra*
water pennyworts (water purslanes),
   Ludwigia spp.
wax myrtle, *Myrica cerifera*
white indigoberry, *Randia aculeata*
white ironwood (boxwood), *Schaef-
   feria fruticens*
white mangrove, *Laguncularia racemosa*
white stopper, *Eugenia axillaris*
white top sedges, Dichromena spp.
white water lily, *Nymphaea odorata*
wild bamboo, *Lasiacis divaricata*
wild banyan, *Ficus brevifolia*
wild cinnamon, *Canella winterana*
wild coffee tree, *Colubrina arbores-
   cens*
wild lime, *Xanthoxylum fagara*
wild olive, *Forestiera segregata*
wild pines (air plants), Tillandsia
   spp., *see* reddish wild pine
wild potatoes, Solanum spp.
wild tamarind, *Lysiloma bahamensis*
willow, *Salix caroliniana*
yellow allamanda, *Urechites lutea*
yellow catopsis, *Catopsis berteron-
   iane*
yellow water lily, *Nymphaea mexicana*
yucca (Spanish dagger), *Yucca aloi-
   folia*

Index

sandspurs, 94
Sangamon period, 81
sarcostemma, 97
sargassum, 85
satinleaf, 97, 152
savannas, 123, 130
savia, 81, 82
saw grass, 47, 54, 72, 76, 111, 115, 120, 122, 125, 126, 127, 128, 130, 135, 141, 143, 157, 165, 167, 179, 180
saw grass marshes, 31, 70, 82, 106, 109, 120, 123, 140, 141, 161, 166, 171
saw grass peat, 113, 163
saw grass sod, 158
saw palmetto, 82, 106, 123, 130, 179, 180
scrub buttonwood, 158, 159
scrub cypress, 170
scrub mangrove, 111, 112
scrub oak, 64, 178
sea blite, 94
sea daisy, 94, 96, 102
sea grape, 82, 94, 101, 105
sea grasses, 81, 85
sea lavender, 94, 106
sea level, 73, 81
sea oats, 94
sea purslane, 94
sedge flats, 144
sedges, 80, 90
seeds, stored, 87, 144
septate bulrush, 138
sesuvium, 94
Seven Palm Lake, 8, 52
seven-year apple, 94
Shark River, 52, 53, 88, 93, 110, 117
Shark River Slough, 3, 47, 50, 56, 67, 124, 126, 127, 136, 164, 166
shell beaches, 43
shell deposits, 79
shell, marine, 85
shell mounds, 2, 11, 94, 97, 98, 105, 177
shinus, 152
shoreline, 36, 41, 91, 94
shortleaf fig, 152
shy leaf, 157
silver palm, 81, 82
Simpson, Charles T., 6, 101, 105, 156
Simpson Hammock, 151

Simpson's stopper, 157
Slagle's Ditch, 4
slash pine, 61, 64, 70
slough, 35, 41, 70, 136, 150, 172
    Madeira, 52
    pineland, 157
    saw grass, 122
Small, J. K., 6, 74, 76
Smith, W. H., 137
Snake Bight Road, 26
snook, 110
soapberry, 97, 101
soils, 59, 119, 149, 172
    Broward, 179
    Charlotte, 179
    Copeland, 179
    Indian, 177
    Keri, 179
    Lakewood, 178
    marl, 35, 57, 61, 65, 68
    Matmon, 179
    organic, 20, 61, 68, 104
    red, 149, 150
    rocky, 61
    sandy, 35, 61, 64
    Suniland, 179
    St. Lucie, 178
solanum, 72
solution holes, 35, 53, 73, 74, 81, 124, 137, 150
Southeast Saline Everglades, 147
Spanish moss, 140
Spanish stopper, 94, 96, 97, 98, 101, 105, 113
spatterdock, 146
spicewood, 70
spider lily, 138, 143, 145
spike moss, 177
spike rush, 125, 135, 143, 144, 145, 171
spike rush marshes, 123, 162, 165, 169
spilanthes, 54, 138
staggerbush, 178, 179
stiff cornel, 175, 176
stoppers, 68. Also *see* red stoppers, Spanish stoppers, and white stoppers
storm tides, 72
strands, 175
submerged meadows, 84
submerged plants, 47
sugarcane, 62

sumac, 152
swamp, 35, 45, 50, 56, 90, 123, 142
   custard apple, 70, 123, 126, 138
swamp fern, 31, 54, 113, 130, 135
swamp hardwood, 56, 127
sweet bay, 54, 130, 135, 137
switch grass, 80
tailgrass, 125
tall sandspur, 87
tamarind. *See* wild tamarind
Tamiami limestone, 33, 35, 61, 62,
   65, 117, 170, 172
Tamiami Trail, 1, 3, 51
tarflower, 179
tarpon, 4
Taylor Slough, 4, 50, 157
temperature, 9-11
Ten Mile Corner, 57
Ten Thousand Islands, 35, 64, 88,
   92, 101
termite, 150
tetrazygia, 152
thatch palm, 81, 82, 83
thoroughwort, 55, 102
Thorne, R. F., 88
tidal lands, 68
topography, 46
torchwood, 82
transpiration, 49, 163
Tree Island Everglades, 61, 162, 164
tree islands, 41, 76, 123, 125, 126,
   142, 162, 166
tree snails, 102, 155
trema, 27
tropical hardwood, 42, 68, 121
tropical hardwood hammocks, 82,
   123, 130, 153, 154, 161, 165,
   170
turtle grass, 84, 85, 91
twinberry, 170, 176, 177
twinflower, 160
twisted air plant, 125
upper keys, 33, 81
U.S. 1, 51, 89

U.S. Soil Conservation Service, 59
varnishleaf, 152
velvetleaf, 81, 177
vine fern, 171
vine orchid, 128
Virginia creeper, 98, 157
Virginia willow, 128, 175
water dropwort, 145
water lettuce, 173, 175
water levels, 141
water lily, 146, 169, 180
water milfoil, 169
water needs, 46
water oak, 64, 170, 173, 175, 176,
   177
water patterns, 49
water pennywort (water purslane),
   54, 55, 138
Watson River, 52
wax myrtle, 54, 70, 98, 116, 135,
   137, 146, 179
West Lake, 6, 8, 26, 52, 109, 120
wet prairies, 65, 144
Whiskey Creek, 56, 121
white indigoberry. *See* randia
white ironwood, 82
white stoppers, 72, 97, 157, 170, 177
Whitewater Bay, 97, 98, 110
white top sedges, 180
wild bamboo, 157
wild cinnamon, 82, 97
wild coffee, 177
wild lime, 72, 98, 105
wild olive, 137
wild tamarind, 81, 82, 170
willow, 54, 126, 135, 137, 143, 163,
   168
willow heads, 45, 68, 70, 76, 121,
   123, 126, 135, 136, 137, 157,
   162, 163, 168
yellow allamanda, 178
yellow catopsis, 125
yucca, 94, 102, 105, 106